THE ART AND PRACTICE
OF ASTRAL PROJECTION

BY

OPHIEL

AUTHOR OF
ART AND PRACTICE OF ASTRAL PROJECTION
ART AND PRACTICE OF GETTING MATERIAL THINGS
THROUGH CREATIVE VISUALIZATION
ART AND PRACTICE OF THE OCCULT
ART AND PRACTICE OF CLAIRVOYANCE
VIGNETTE LESSONS IN OCCULT POWER
CORRESPONDENCE COURSE IN THE FOUNDATIONS
OF OCCULT KNOWLEDGE
CORRESPONDENCE COURSE IN ASTRAL PROJECTION
ORACLE OF FORTUNA

SAMUEL WEISER, INC.
York Beach, Maine

First published 1961
Nineteenth printing 1982

Copyright © Edward Peach, 1961

ISBN 0-87728-246-3

Samuel Weiser, Inc.
P.O. Box 612
York Beach, Maine 03910

Printed in U.S.A. by
NOBLE OFFSET PRINTERS, INC.
New York, N.Y. 10003

—DEDICATION—

This book is lovingly dedicated to Ophiel's mean, violent, and stubborn disposition! Because of his innate stubborness Ophiel never gave up no matter how bad things were or how contemptible the failure was. If it had not been for this stubborness, however, Ophiel would have laid down and died from sheer mortification and disappointment many years ago. Ophiel was assigned a job in this world before he was born. His job was to bring Occult knowledge thru and to give PRACTICAL TEACHINGS AND INSTRUCTIONS IN ITS USE FOR THE BENEFIT OF OCCULT STUDENTS. Ophiel was not allowed this knowledge before hand and to force him into the path, and to keep him in the path, all material things were taken away from him as one takes a baby's toys away when it comes time for it to do things other than play. In addition everybody and everything, were forced to let him down; and let him down violently and in a particularly stupid manner. All plans, all dreams, all desires, all projects, were made to fail in a very silly looking way so that it appeared very funny to strangers, his friends and relatives. He was not even allowed alcohol or nicotine (and just barely coffee and tea) to alleviate these painful mental blows but had to take it-sweating it out without any help.

However the object of all this was to force him to turn to his Inner resources and to conquer all with nothing but his own Inner. This was done and the Inner resources are now working.

This book is the first fruits of the Inner Workings. Ophiel hopes you will value it if only for what it cost him to produce it.

FOREWORD AND INTRODUCTION

In the major Arcana of the pack of Tarot Cards there is a card, number 18, called "The Moon"

This Tarot card portrays, starting at the bottom of the card and proceeding upward, first, a pool of water, then a shore lined with some rocks and plants. A path starts at the edge of the pool and winds up thru the middle of the card and ends off to the left upper top side of the card.

At the start of the path and just coming out of the water is a crayfish. In the foreground of the scene are two animals, one, a wolf, is on the right side of the path and the other, a dog, is on the left side of the path.

In the middle of the card-scene is a wall with a gap in the middle thru which the path passes. On each side of the gap is a high tower. The wall and the towers symbolize the boundry between the physical plane and the Astral plane.

As you can see the path leads from the physical plane on thru the gap between the two towers and into the Astral plane. This is the path of progress for man. If man follows the ordinary progress of advancement he should, in course of time, enter these inner planes freely, and that while still living in the physical body.

Most all books in the world deal with the land before the wall. A few occult books deal with the land beyond the wall. And hardly any at all, as far as the author has been able to find out, after a long search, deals with *how* to enter, and travel thru the Astral plane, in safety, and return to the physical plane, at will.

This book, an occult book, deals with the subject of how to enter this Astral plane, function there, and then return to the physical plane, with a great deal of memory-knowledge of the "trip" retained in the memory and available for study and research. This book is a practical Occult book in that it gives all the theory necessary to understand the subject AND THE DEFINITE DIRECTION PRACTICES AS TO HOW TO DO IT. Not only does it give positive directions but it gives FOUR different methods of dealing with the Inner Planes.

This book contains all you need to make a definite start in the working of the Art of Astral Projection.

Strangely enough, in all inner plane matters, it appears, from the material standpoint, that it is the preparation that counts most and not the doing, after the preparation, that counts.

This book places a great deal of emphasis on the preparations, as you will notice, and if you will follow these directions for the preliminary work you will have a very good chance of succeeding in learning how to make a definite inner plane projection that will delight and satisfy you.

Then when you have mastered the techniques as given in this book and you feel that you are ready for more advanced work, contact Ophiel; and it is planned that by that time more advanced work will be available for students. I was originally going to include some work of an advanced nature in this book but it was pointed out to me that this might confuse the new student and he might try something before he had sufficient experience to carry out the operation and the resulting failure would discourage him.

Therefore this book deals with beginning work only and, as said before, when you are ready contact Ophiel and indicate your interest in advanced work along these lines. So good luck to you and may you succeed.

Ophiel

Additional New Foreword and Introduction.

A number of years have passed since the first edition of Art and Practice of Astral Projection appeared.

In spite of the limitations of Ophiel's ability to distribute and promote this book, the book has been as well received as can be expected under the circumstances.

It all sort of comes back to the coming of the Aquarian Age when, hopefully, all sorts of good things will happen to replace the dastardly goings on of the Piscian Age, which rules, among other undesirable things, prisons, restrictions, and such like.

One good use the book seemed to have was to assist many people, who were in advance of the Age, and were already projecting naturally. Their natural projections were accompanied by definite physical symptoms which symptoms looked very strange to others and even took on the appearance of insanity!! So much so, that the student was afraid to consult a doctor or psychologist for fear of being thought going insane. When the student, however, read in the Art and Practice of Astral Projection about the symptoms of first projections efforts he could recognize and identify those effects in himself, and be reasonably assured he was on the right path. This assistance brought a great deal of relief to many students for which I am glad to have been of help.

Ophiel receives a constantly increasing number of letters from young persons sixteen, fourteen, and even twelve years old who seem to be projecting quite naturally. It would seem that the next coming generation once removed will be projecting as a matter of course, a fact of daily life living and probably manifesting all kinds of other psychic facilities which are not usually apparent.

Many changes have taken place in the last few years, not the least of which are changes in social attitudes towards old taboos. It is a peculiar characteristic of monotheistic religions that they desire to FORCE their ONE GOOD IDEA onto others — all the way down from Akhenaton to Puritans. The old religions of multiple Gods and Goddesses were tolerant of each other and persecutions for religious ideas were unknown.

SECTIONS

REGARDING THE COLOR ON THE COVER

The colors on the cover of this book are the colors you will "see" just before you "break thru" into the Astral plane with your newly developed clairvoyant Inner sight gained thru the work given in this book.

When you "see" these colors you will know you are making progress.

The first thing to appear is the solid black. Then the colors begin to appear thru the black as is shown where the colors are lined in-between with black. The black then thins out and away and the colors become more brilliant and finally burst out into the blinding pure white Astral Light.

Little System

There is no subject, of the Occult, that has attracted more attention from Occult students than the subject of Astral Projection. No greater achievement, in Occult arts, seems more desirable than that achievement of being able to leave the physical body — in full consciousness — "travel out" in the material, and the immaterial world, invisible, undetectable, able to go anywhere and everywhere without let or hinderance, observing persons, actions, events, freely — then returning to the physical body with full memory of the "trip-projection". In addition, to this generally accepted concept of Astral Projection, Occult novels and semi-serious-occult literature are full of wonderful stories of students, who had mastered this Art, and their adventures as they roamed around the earth and even went to other planets!!! Truly the ability to project Astrally is something greatly to be desired.

But what drives the poor ordinary occult student mad with frustration is that when he looks in those same occult books to find out *HOW TO LEARN TO PROJECT* he finds nothing about that part of the subject. No Directions! Not even a basic occult theory to guide him. All that the occult books generally have to say is that when he is "ready" he will find out how to do it or they might say that when he finds his "master" the master will teach him how to do it.

To the real earnest occult student, anxious to make true progress in this Art, this kind of talk is for the birds.

It should seem that there would be some ordinary information available, on this subject, so that the earnest student could at least prepare himself somewhat along these lines until his master shows up; or, if the master never comes, to be able to try to learn at least the basic rudiments of the Projection Art by himself.

Now I want to be honest with you from the start so that you will always trust me to give you sound Occult knowledge and safe practices,—in this book, and in the others I hope to write and I hope you will buy and read. So I will tell you now that knowledge on any Occult subject, that you are seeking, is available now somewhere in an Occult book; and not necessarily out-of-print or high priced either. There seems to be some kind of an Occult law about this. I am telling you this so that you will understand that I am not claiming to be the sole giver-out-of-occult-knowledge that so many other teachers claim to be. So I will repeat again-*any* and *all* Occult knowledge that you are searching for is down in occult books somewhere and many of these books have been in print for 500 years or more!

Therefore to get accurate Occult knowledge and practices you must search for them. There are three factors that govern this search however. One factor is that you have to look for the right books and put out some money to buy them. Two factor is that you must have a minimum amount of Occult experience and knowledge to be able to recognize true Occult Knowledge when you see it printed. And factor three is that you must have a minimum amount of Occult experience to be able to apply this knowledge to make the best use of it. Thus accurate Occult knowledge, including the knowledge of Astral Projection, is scattered throughout many different kinds of books and you will have to cover the field and read many of them to get out all the pieces and put them together yourself. This is the only time when a teacher, like me, can help you. I have covered this field for 30 years and, by hard work, I have accumulated the necessary Occult knowledge and practices. I can give you both the knowledge and practices as fast as you can learn them.

In this little book I am going to give you all the necessary information about the Art of Astral Projection, as well as simple and concise directions, on how to practice the Art in a safe and sane manner. I am going to give you not just one method but four methods. These four methods will differ from each other in ranging from the very easy to the very hard and with various degrees of intensity of application needed. You will learn each method progressively in turn and the experience you gain in the first method will carry over into the other following methods. If you will give close attention to the text and follow directions carefully, and patiently, you should learn a great deal about this Art and many of you will master it. Everyone will need some personal instructions and you will find, in the last section of this book, directions how to contact me personally for this personal instruction. In studying this book and in following instructions you are on the right path for results. I respectfully suggest that you stick to me for the teacher and the book for the master until you have finished it and achieved some degree of success in this Art.

There are some other important things that you should know, and understand thoroughly, before you start actual work on the systems of projection that I am giving you in this book. Most of the troubles and disappointments that come from Occult studies are due to a misunderstanding of the following matters. Please read and study the following information until you understand it throughly.
THEN FOLLOW IT.

First — I want you to understand that work in and on the Occult is of the nature of an Art, and must be considered and practiced as such. Do you know what an Art is? as against a trade? Let us consider, for an example, a painter of pictures as against a painter of houses. At first glance there is a slight similarity in that they both use paints and brushes and apply this material to a surface, and, in a way, they are both called painters. Then the similarity ceases. As you know the painter of houses can be almost anyone who has the strength and physical ability to be able to move a brush full of paint material against a surface of some kind. The artist — painter does not require strength of much capacity as he applies paint to a rather small surface. The painter of houses does not use his own ideas as to how the house should be painted but follows directions of others. A painter of pictures follows no one's directions but follows his own ideas entirely as to what to paint down on his canvas. Almost anyone can learn to paint a house but only a few can be an artist — painter. One house painter paints like most any other but no artist paints like another artist but is very different and individualistic. A house painter must please others with his work but an artist pleases only himself and may displease everyone else. A man can be a real artist only if

3

he can open his inner being and let the basic creative instincts come out and express themselves, regardless of what others think, or want, and regardless of the consequences.

So to practice Astral Projection, and/or the Occult Arts, you have to have two things—One, Have something of the Soul of an Artist in you and then be able to let it out in expression. Everyone has a little of the artist in him and in practising the Occult Arts you must strive to let it out as freely as you can. You must do as the artist does — perfect a technique of an Art — and then let your inner being out to use the technique. In the degree that you can do this is the degree of your successful powers of welding the Occult Forces. We cannot all be Leonardo da Vincis but we can all learn *something* about Art and we can learn to express it in our own little way, which may turn out to be a lot or a little, but always more than nothing. And you might perfect this Art of Astral Projection yourself to a great ability.

And the Second thing is — You should know that no thing in the physical-world-universe is what it is supposed to be, or is, according to what people think it is. This is especially true about the Inner Planes. Everything about the Inner Planes is different than what it is supposed or thought to be. Different from what the churches say it is — different from what the spiritualists say it is. On the one hand there are certain widely held ideas that are true and also there are certain fundamental things that are true. On the other hand there are many widely held ideas that are not true and many fundamental conceptions that are not true. In many cases when the theory is wrong the thing still works. In many cases things do not work because basic theory is wrong but would work if a little knowledge was introduced. Many times a thing works, as I said, BUT NOT BECAUSE OF THE REASON THAT IS GIVEN FOR IT WORKING AND WITH THE RESULTS THAT YOU MIGHT EXPECT.

The Occult Art of Astral Projection is definitely one of the above designated things. Astral Projections do work BUT NOT WITH THE RESULTS YOU EXPECT, because the Inner Planes are not what you thought they were or were taught they were. THE INNER PLANES ARE QUITE DIFFERENT THAN WHAT THEY ARE THOUGHT TO BE. So I suggest you forget what

4

you have been TOLD the inner planes are like or speculate on what you are going to see and experience — learn the Art — practice the Art — and follow where the results lead. You will then KNOW what the inner planes are like from first hand personal knowledge and not from hearsay.

At this point I will make the second reference to the last section of this book. In the last section of this book I intend to refer to many things of an advanced nature in connection with the four systems that I am giving you now. However I do not intend to *give* material of an advanced nature in this book at this time. I will make some references to advanced work with each of the systems as we go along and it will be necessary for you to contact me personally (1960) to get this advanced work as I will have to be satisfied that you are ready for it but only that you do not undertake something that you are not prepared to handle, and not that I want to withhold information from you or sell it to you for a high price. In case that this book lasts for many years, as I hope it will, I will try to arrange for a successor to carry on after me.

With these preliminary things out of the way we are now ready to take up the practical study and practice of the Art of Astral Projection. I am going to divide the instructions into two parts — The Basic Theory Part and the Basic-Practical-Working part.

Part 1. BASIC THEORY —

As I said it is not my intention, nor is it possible in this little book, to go too deeply into the entire subject of Occult Knowledge. I will therefore confine myself to the basic-occult pertaining to the Art of Astral Projection and will give you all that is necessary to lay a sensible foundation for the practical work to follow. I am assuming that, as you have bought this book, you have some knowledge of the Occult already. I will, therefore, make a rather short review of certain limited Occult knowledge, at this point, and I trust these things will be familiar to you. If they are not familiar to you then it will be necessary for some of you to read up — research along these lines. If the material is familiar to you it would still be a good idea for you to review this basic material again anyhow sometime before you start active practice.

The Theosophical books written by Anne Besant and C. W. Leadbeater are full of information about the inner planes and man's inner bodies. To mention a few — "The Hidden Side of Things" "The Chakras" The books by Col. Powell — "The Etheric Body", "The Astral Body" "The Mental Body", The Causual Body". Most all the books published by the branch of the Theosophical Society whose headquarters is in Adyar, Madras, India and whose American Headquarters is in Wheaton Illinois — contain valuable information about the inner planes. There will be a number of helpful books listed at the end of this book. Get and read as many of them as you can.

So we will assume that you are an Occult student who has studied for some time along these lines and thus you should have learned that a man is more than just a physical body and another "thing" called a Soul. You should have learned, or at least heard, that a man consists of a number of "things" called "Bodies" A Physical body, an Etheric body, an Astral body, (a higher Astral body and a lower Astral body) a Mental body and a Causal body. And probably some other "things" too.

Now it is true that the noun "body" applied to these "bodies" does not mean the same thing as it does when it is applied to the physical body. But there is really no other good word to use except "centers of consciousness" which is true but then there is also a certain kind of organization about each of these centers and for that reason they can be called bodies too. The English language is not very rich in words describing the higher things and for this reason there is much confusion about the finer points of many meanings. In this book I will put these marks "—" before and after a word and when I do this you are to give it another look as to its meaning.

As you can then see, for yourself, a man is not just a physical body and a something called a "soul" He has, or it appears that he has, several different kinds of other body-centers, called bodies too.

At this point we might as well start looking at that thing which is called a "Soul" and see if we can pin "it" down and take a look at "it". As none of these other bodies can rightly be called a soul (body) they do not appear to be the soul that we are looking for. The soul must be something above all of these other bodies. As there is no very good definition of a Soul in Occult literature that fits the facts, as one who knows about it from experience of the inner type, we turn to the dictionary and see if we can find anything there to help us.

The dictionary is not of much help either. The dictionary says that the word Soul means Spirit and when we turn to Spirit we find that the dictionary says the word Spirit means Soul!!!! (also it is rather strange to find that the word Ghost means Soul and/or Spirit!)

Therefore to get on with our study I will tell you that we have to turn to Alchemy to get the meaning of the word Soul. The word Soul means Spirit and the word Spirit means AIR!!! However this is not ordinary Air but means the Quality of Air (no relation to the physical Air other than in a very superficial way) The quality of Air is MOTION — or AIR IN MOTION. ANYTHING THAT MOVES IS ALIVE THEREFORE THE QUALITY OF LIFE IS MOTION — not motion as such but MOTION IN THE SENSE OF LIFE-MOVEMENT — the ability to life-live and move.

So therefore the SOUL QUALITY of a man is living, the ACTION OF LIVING and of course this quality does go beyond the bodies that are merely the vehicles of living-life.

So you can see plainly that the basic meaning of Soul and Spirit are grossly misinterpreted and are used wrongly by all religious bodies. As Soul and Spirit are wrongly used and as they have no bearing on the Art of Astral Projection, which is what we are studying here, these two words will not be used in this book any further. I would also suggest that you be very careful as to how you use them in the future as if you are going to learn Occult Knowledge you have to say exactly what you mean at all times.

So let us start out again in our study of the Art of Astral Projection by asking ourselves — What, exactly, is meant by the term "Astral Projection" What, exactly, are we talking about when we use these words?

The ordinary everyday idea of this term "Astral Projection" is — A man separates "something" of himself from his physical body and with this "something" goes "out" somewhere, and then returns to his physical body with full memory knowledge of where he has been and what he has done. This would be the ordinary idea about

7

this term Astral Projection.

In the case of an advanced Occult Student who has made such a successful Astral Projection — what has happened — theoretically and practically???

Well we now know that he did not travel "out" as a "spirit" in a "thing" called a "spiritual" body, so what did he travel out in? and what was "it" called? It also follows that it was not to or on a thing called the "spiritual" plane that he went to or traveled on. Yet it appears that it was with some kind of an inner body and to some kind of an inner plane that he went to and with.

Now here is a very important matter. In fact the following information is the heart of Astral Projection. I discovered this myself and therefore I am free to tell you about it freely.

It should be relatively plain to you, by now, that a man consists of more than one "body" and also that there exists more than one plane. You, as a man, possesses a number of bodies thru and in which you function, and have functioned, all your physical life. Each of these bodies has a "plane" corresponding to it and thru which it draws certain things that make up your life on this physical plane. Therefore you are no stranger to these bodies and to these planes! It is said that in and during sleep you have always left the physical body and done many things and went many places. This is an old Occult doctrine. (In the second system that I give to you in this book this sleep projection will be made much clearer to you so if you don't fully understand the above wait until you study the second system).

IF THE ABOVE IS TRUE WHY DON'T YOU REMEMBER YOUR NIGHTLY PROJECTIONS?- THE *REASON WHY YOU DON'T REMEMBER IS THAT THE BULK OF YOUR CONSCIOUSNESS IS IN THE PHYSICAL BODY* AND REMAINS THERE MOST ALL YOUR LIFE *UNLESS YOU CONSCIOUSLY TRANSFER IT ELSEWHERE*!!!!

AND NOW YOU HAVE THE SECRET OF ASTRAL PROJECTION in a nut shell. YOU DO NOT PROJECT AN ETHERIC BODY OR AN ASTRAL BODY. *YOU DO NOT PROJECT ANYTHING. ALL YOU DO IS TO TRANSFER CONSCIOUSNESS TO ANOTHER BODY OTHER THAN THE*

PHYSICAL.

That is what you are going to do in the four systems that I am going to give to you in this book. YOU ARE GOING TO LEARN TO PROJECT YOUR CONSCIOUSNESS TO THE BODY YOU HAVE THAT CORRESPONDS TO THE BODY OF THE PLANE YOU WANT TO GO TO.

However for all practical purposes you can consider the action as a projection, and it is a kind of a projection — a *projection* of *consciousness* however instead of a "body". We will, therefore, continue to refer to our work as projection and speak as if we project a body etc.

For the purposes of your study, and I hope that you will take my word for it now until you do your own research on the matter, there are only three planes that you can "project" too. The first of these planes, and the nearest to the physical body-plane, is the Etheric plane. The next plane, and a little farther away from the physical plane yet very close to it, is the lower Astral. The next plane and still farther away from the physical plane is the higher Astral. Now there are still higher planes than these, of course, but in those higher planes all FORMS begin to "thin" out so there is really nothing to which to project to in those higher planes. These higher planes, and your higher bodies that correspond to them, are really nothing but abstract principles, you *ARE THEM*. However they can be contacted but this is another advanced study for which see the last section.

I will give a very brief description of each of the planes with which we are concerned with in this book. If this description does not contain enough information so that you can understand the plane fully I suggest, as I said before, that you take my word for it now until you can do your own research on it later. I believe I can give you enough practical information now as to enable you to work with the plane for the time being and to recognize it when your consciousness is transfered to it.

I am going to start with the physical plane which is really the very first plane and which you might think you are throughly familiar with, but there are still many things that you, and others, do not know about your physical plane — body and its possibilities.

9

The physical body is the final instrument of all the other planes, the end result as it were, and it is of this fact that we do not know how to take full advantage of! It is on the physical plane that we can reap the advantage of things started on the inner planes and can enjoy them fully. One of the Occult teachings regardings the planes is that a man cannot take fullest advantage of any one plane until he has gained some knowledge, and CONTROL, of the plane above that one — we cannot fully use any one plane until we have some power on the plane above that one. — I repeat we cannot fully use any one plane until we have some power on the plane above it. The reason for this is that each plane is positive to the one below and negative to the one above it. Thus, naturally, in the work you are starting — learning to practice the Art of Astral Projection — you have to start with and from the physical plane. I want to call to your attention, at this time, that even if you never learn to project at all — not likely — this study is going to do you a great deal of good in *Living this physical life*.

As I said before the higher planes control the lower planes. In addition to learning this Art of projection you are going to have to enter the inner planes, more especially at first the Etheric Plane, and in this way, as a side line to your projection work, you will learn about these planes, and if you pay attention to the work you should develop a *marked degree of control over the physical plane*. This knowledge and power will enable you to "work" down from the Etheric plane to control the physical. I will speak of this more in the last section. For the time being keep in mind that the physical plane is the end plane of a number of "inner" planes, and what you "DO" on the inner planes determines the final "effect" on the outer physical. *You cannot recall — remember* this *too much*.

To proceed — The next plane "above" the physical plane is the Etheric plane. You have an Etheric body which you probably are not too aware of. However you "use" your Etheric body constantly and continually. Rather, to make it clearer, you might say that you use your Etheric body every second of your physical life-living. For purposes of understanding this more you can picture the physical body as of a sort of honeycomb-like construction and the Etheric body fills those honeycomb-like cells like honey fills the ordinary honeycomb.

There are ways in which the Etheric body can be seen with the physical eyes so near is it to the physical body. If the eyes are trained by looking thru a piece of glass stained with a certain dye of a certain color, it is then possible to see the Etheric body surrounding the physical body like a kind of white shadow commonly called an Aura. If the eyes are treated this way for some time carefully they then become accumstomed to seeing this Aura by looking for it. (further information on this in the last section)

As I said previously your consciousness is now centered in the Physical Body and it is for this reason that you are not aware of the existence of these other bodies. You will become aware of them shortly as you learn to expand your consciousness to the other bodies each in turn.

The Etheric body is so close to the physical body that you can become aware of it physicaly. The next time you ascend or descend in a very fast elevator note the "sinking" feeling that you have in the "pit" of your stomach. This sinking feeling is due to the Etheric Body moving out of contact with the physical body due to the pressure of the rapid movement of the elevator. The Etheric Body is just on the border line of solid and just enough so that it is effected by this type of physical pressure.

There is a type of magical work that enables a man to get control of his Etheric Body. So much so that he can do many strange and powerful things with the Etheric Body on the physical plane. It is possible during certain times of the 24 hour period of a day to "thicken" the Etheric Body so that it can be seen and felt by others. The Egyptians had develcped this type of magic to a great degree. They had a very common symbol for this Etheric double or Ka as they called it. The symbol was two uplifted arms joined in the middle where the shoulders would be. If you are interested in this sort of thing contact me as per directions in the last section of this book.

However people's bodies are somewhat different in these times. For example in the old days very few persons had too much food and that was not too nourishing in many ways. A physical body that is part starved all the time is rather loosely connected with its Etheric Body and the separation is rather easy. A healthly well fed well nourished physical body is very tightly connected with its Etheric double. However you can practice for a time a rigid diet and achieve some results. However don't expect too much.

To continue — The Etheric Body can be effected by mental thoughts and strong emotions as you might surmise. Extra strong physical shocks can disrupt it and tear it loose from the physical body entirely as you might guess from the elevator example. During the last war many people were found dead in London without a physical mark on them. A bomb had exploded nearby and the combination of fear, shock, and terrific vibration had driven the Etheric Body out of the Physical Body so far that it could not reestablish connections, as it could do in the elevator example when the lighter pressure was removed by the stopping of the ride.

So much for the Etheric plane. The amount of knowledge I have given you here by no means exhausts the knowledge available about this plane. (You would do well to get the books that I have referred to heretofore and start your own research into this plane). However as you are now starting to work with this plane you will study it as you go along.

The "body" "above" the Etheric body is the Astral Body and the plane above the Etheric Plane is the Astral Plane. The Astral Plane is much more important than the Etheric Plane in that this plane has a much more wider application to the Physical Universe than the Etheric Plane. The Etheric plane is somewhat personal in its application to you and is small, narrow, and limited. The Astral Plane is very "large" and contains much more of a variety of things than any of the other planes. Many more of Nature's Forces course thru this plane than any of the other planes and their application is widely distributed; whereas the forces, by the time they enter the Etheric Plane began to become individualized and personalized.

The Astral Plane differs from all other planes in another respect in that there is a Lower Astral and a Higher Astral. The lowest part of the Astral Plane is very much like the Etheric where they come together and the highest part of the Astral Plane is very much like the Mental Plane where they come together. None of the other planes

12

have lower and higher levels so well marked. The Etheric is the Etheric and the Mental is the Mental but the Astral contains elements of each of these two planes all mixed up which is what makes this plane so fascinating. The Astral plane must be entered into very carefully, and with absolutely the correct technique, or there can be trouble of an annoying nature.

Forms, such as they are, on the Astral Plane are very fluid in that they flow about and change shapes and appearances very easily and quickly. As basic forces have a wide play on the Astral Plane there is much color which is the Force itself. All Astral forms are composed of many points of colors so much that the realm is called the Star plane or Astral which means star. The forms near the "bottom" of the lower Astral partake of the nature of the Etheric Plane and so are more stable but still show the star-like effect which is the signature as it were, of the Astral Plane.

On the higher Astral "forms" have practically no form at all but colors take over completely as the Astral blends into the Mental plane. The Mental plane is the plane of forces and has absolutely no form or forms at all. The entire Mental realm plane is all colors which are vibrations themselves.

There is a type of magic in which a person can enter this Mental plane with a form made up of lower matter. The "form" being brought "up" from "below" as it were. Or to explain it to make it fully clear — A form is organized on a much lower plane and then this form is "taken" up into the Mental plane. When this is done properly a great deal of powerful work can be accomplished by the operator. (Again this belongs to advanced work but it seems such a proper place to let people know about it and what can be done. When you are ready contact me about this advanced work)

You possess an Astral body, of course, but there is no material way that you can become aware of it as you can of the etheric body. It will not be possible for you to see the Astral body until you are advanced enough to take and succeed in one of the advanced courses mentioned in this book in the last section.

The Astral body and the Astral plane are very tricky to "work" with and require some experience as to what you are doing and how

13

to do it. It would never do to enter this plane without having definite experience in some kind of lesser projection work first. The method I am going to give you to start this work with is admirable for gaining this necessary experience.

You also possess a Mental body and a Causal body. Not too much can be said about them (and certainly not in this little book). *YOU ARE THEM* — The Mental body and the Causal body are not used for projection-traveling so as this book is primarily about projections these bodies will not be mentioned further.

At this point I believe it will be of help to you for me to stop and make a brief summary of what we have covered up to now. If you do not grasp the information fully I am again asking you to take my word for these things until you are able to do your own studies and research on them and experience them yourself.

We now know that a man has several other bodies besides the physical body. We now know that each of these bodies has a plane to correspond with it, and it is on these corresponding planes that the corresponding body consciousness projects to: from the physical plane, as a base, as the physical plane is where our consciousness is centered now.

We have found that the Etheric and Mental Planes are quite distinct by themselves from the others but the Astral Plane is one of gradual change from the lowest part to the highest part. We have found that the lowest Astral resembles the Etheric Plane, to which it joins on the lower part, and the highest Astral resembles the Mental plane, to which it joins on the upper part. We now know that the Astral plane is the "largest" of the planes and that it has more differences in it than similarities. (Actually there is no such thing as largeness, smallness, up, down, sideways or anything like that on the Astral plane or, indeed, on any plane except the physical. However it is necessary to use ordinary English language in describing this work. Hence, as said before whenever a word is put in these marks "—" then look out for deeper meanings for which there are no good English words.)

We have found that, due to its interesting complexities, the Astral Plane has attracted most of the attention of those who want to practice

14

the Art of Projection. We have found that projections can be made with both Etheric and Astral bodies. We have found that while we live and move in all our bodies at the same time our consciousness is centered in the physical body for now. We have found that instead of really "projecting", as it seems we do, we are merely transfering our personal consciousness to another body and living and moving in that body, the same as we do now in the physical body. As most projectors end up projecting to the Astral plane and as Etheric projections require special work for limited objectives, and is really on the borderline between the Etheric and the Astral anyhow, we will, after this, in refering to projections mean only Astral projections and discard all other kinds, except when specially stated. I did, however, feel that I should mention the Etheric and upper and lower Astrals as all the other teachers leave them out entirely (they probably don't know about them) and the student should know what he is doing at all times. Many times projections are different and the student can recognize from the character of the "scenery" what plane he is on.

In my work, in the past, teaching Astral projection certain questions come up time and time again. In fact I recall that these same questions bothered me when I was starting out. I have decided therefore to group all these questions together here now and to answer them at one time. The questions in the order of their frequency are:—

1. Why don't other writers give exact directions as to the practice of the Art of Astral projection the same as you do?
2. Is it wrong to learn the Art of Projection?
3. Is it hard to learn this Art?
4. Is there more than one way to project?
5. What results can I expect to achieve by learning this Art?
6. What can one expect to "see" "over" "there"?

These are all natural important questions and they should be answered before you start to do the actual work. So I will answer them in order.

The first question:— Why don't other writers give exact directions as to the practice of Astral projections the same as you do?

15

The answer to this question is — Our Solar system, in making its rounds about the belt of the Zodiac, has entered the House of Aquarius. This means that the old age of Pisces has passed away. The Aquarian forces are better than the Piscesan forces which, among other things, stood for prisons, and the world has certainly been in prison for the past 2000 years. That age is now past and the people are responding to this new age ruled by Uranus who is a higher Saturn in a sense. Now-a-days the psychic-etheric powers of people are awakening spontaneously. Many people are having psychic experiences and many other people are projecting naturally: and do not know the reason for it, or what it means, and are looking for explanations. Thus people are ready for Occult study and training.

In olden times people were not ready for this work in large numbers but only as individuals would ready themselves to receive advanced knowledge. Then these individuals had to seek out those who could give them this advanced knowledge (there are always teachers around somewhere) This was what I was refering to when I made the early reference to old books in which the writer tells how his MASTER showed him how to work Astral projection etc.

Therefore when a person acquired this knowledge, and other occult knowledge, from a teacher he was put under oath not reveal this knowledge to anyone else freely. Again this kind of teaching-knowledge was given out by secret societies as part of their training for their members and the kinds of oaths they had to take were terrific not to revel the knowledge to outsiders. So when one of these people would write a book they would tell ABOUT IT but not TELL IT. For example the book called "Practical Astral Projection" by Yram, which is Mary spelled backward, (why I'll never know) he tells about WHAT he did but makes only a vague reference as to HOW IT WAS DONE. I, fortunately, thru working 30 years on Occult studies, and neglecting all other important things, had accumulated enough Occult knowledge and Occult practice-knowledge, the hard way, to be able to recognize his coy hint and therefore I know how he did it. But I trust, you understand, that I got this knowledge myself thru my own meditation efforts and therefore I am under no obligation not to reveil it and so I do.

Question 2 — Is it wrong to learn to project Astrally?

This strange question comes up many times, more than you would think it would. I, myself, never felt anything right or wrong about projection one way or another anymore than I would feel it was wrong to paint pictures or carve statues. There are people in this world to whom Art is "wikkid" and many other things, of which they know nothing about or do not have under their control, they consider "bad" or wrong. But in this modern Aquarian age they are getting pushed into the limbo of forgotten things as they deserve to be.

It is true that these Occult 'things are of the new age and, as a rule, it is equally true that only certain kinds of people will practice them during the early part of their presentation before the masses take them up. The early users of anything new have to be of an unconventional nature in order to even notice new things. This type of person is apt to experiment too much with other conventions such as sex and other taboos. And it is these things that gets the old maids and old foggies all upset.

Try to take the learning of this Art in your stride and avoid doing other things in an unconventional manner. However these old foggies' loud cries do make many people worry about whether they might be doing something wrong. I have heard the argument advanced that with developing these powers some persons would take an unfair advantage of other people who do not develop their powers. Well the answer to that is that the work is open to all who want to do it and if they don't believe in it and will have nothing to do with developing their powers they are in the same position as anyone who will not advance with the times. This is a new age, as I said, and those who will not advance with the new age can go their own way for all I can care about them. The factory which will not install modern machinery is always at a disadvantage against the factory that has the latest up-to-date machines in it and the old fashioned mind is no match for the modern intelligence. If you have these kind of doubts I guess it is something you will have to battle out for yourself. My assurance is not your assurance. Like most of the ideas of the world this idea is wrong. But all I can say is that I do not think it is wrong to learn the Art of Projection and any or all other Occult Arts. There are uses of these Arts that are questionable but this is a matter for the individual to work out for himself after he learns the Art.

Question 3 — Is it hard to learn the Art of Projection?

As I said before you have always lived in and used these other bodies all your life. Actually you know, unconsciously, how to use the other bodies so this is not what you learn to do. What you do learn to do is to transfer your consciousness to these other bodies and RETAIN MEMORY of the transfer. Your quickness in transfering over depends upon your grasp of the basic principles and then following directions accurately as to practices in the courses I offer. If you have done a great deal of occult study of all kinds of occult books, from the very simple to the very complex, that study would be of great help to you to master these practices. I should hesitate to say how long it would take one who was totally unfamiliar with the Occult to accomplish this Art. But then again I would feel optimistic about a person who did not know very much about the Occult yet had a burning desire to succeed in this Art. And then again I would have doubts about a person who knew a great deal about the Occult yet just dabbled around in it. A short time ago I dropped in at a place in Southern California that had once been a very active occult society led by a man, who was said to be a good psychic and was a good writer on Occult subjects. After his death there has been a steady decline in the activities of the group until now they look as if they are just waiting to be covered over. I talked with a woman working there (1960) who told me she had been there since 1918 - 40 years!! I asked her, among other things, if she had developed clairvoyance and could project Astrally etc. Her reply was that SHE DID NOT WANT ANY THING LIKE THAT! So here is a woman who has been sitting around an occult center for 40 years and wants no development of her latent powers! So she never got any! What an advertisement for the place! Why would she hang around an occult center for 40 years if she does not want anything from it? She might as well have stayed at home and washed dishes for all the good it did her.

So the real answer to this question is — If you want it you'll get it. If you don't want it you won't get it. And this is true of anything in the world.

Question 4 — Is there more than one way to project?

The answer is — Yes there are quite a few different ways to project and many variations in each way. The differences in ways are also the differences in what kind of projections you want to make. If you want to make an Etheric Projection, that is one way. If you want to make an Astral Projection that is another way. There are also obscure ways that I have heard about but never used myself as they over-lapped the other ways.

As I felt that this subject was new to my readers, even those who know something about the occult, I decided to confine myself to four strong courses which I shall describe below. I will name them at this time and describe them more fully later. These four do not exhaust all possible work along these lines. When you finish these courses and master them and still want more I will be available to give still more advanced work by personal contact.

In this book

For practical work in Astral projection I offer the following courses —

1. The "Little" method.
2. The "Dream" method.
3. The "Body of Light" method.
4. The Symbol System method.

Again I am not going to claim that I am the sole repository of Occult Knowledge on these things as other teachers do. With the exception of the "little" course, which I discovered and developed myself, all these things are in Occult books and have been for many hundreds of years. I did, however, work them over and rearrange them, in modern terms, and I give supervisory directions upon personal contact as to how to best study them and I watch the student to see that it is done as near correct as possible as every person is slightly different in their reactions. It does require a degree of experience and plenty of occult knowledge and theory for me to steer a student thru these courses. To know when to tell him to do more and to tell him to do less. To encourage him when he runs into one of those spells when no Occult work can be done successfully and to tell him why.

A certain amount of Occult knowledge is absolutely necessary for the successful practice of this work. Until you can get this for yourself it is very hard to make progress. Therefore it is vitally necessary to have an experienced person to help you thru the first stages of this great work. The Occult is full of double talk for the reasons that I gave you before. Yet those big teachers did not want to leave the field entirely void of practical working knowledge in case some did develop by themselves, which they do all the time. The Masters therefore wrote many books in which they put down certain things partly but leave out much more. Then, as I said, when a man reaches a certain development he recognizes this hidden truth and uses it.

For example — In the collected works of Paracelsus there is an account about creating a homoculus, or an artificial man, out of the elements as it were. Everyone has assumed that this meant the creation of a little physical man of water, earth, fire, and air. A test tube man as it were. Even the great writer Sommerset Maghum in his novel The Magician has Oliver Haddo creating a deformed little monster in a bottle.

Well, as I said, it takes a large amount-degree of Occult knowledge to know what this is all about. This Homoculus legend is a perfect example of Occult hidden-knowledge that is so frustrating to the beginner until he begins to understand.

What does Paracelsus actually mean in this legend? What is he talking about? I am going to tell you what he means but you will have to take my word for it now until you can do your own work on it and then you will KNOW and do not have to take anyone's word for it.

WHAT THEY ARE TALKING ABOUT IS THE CREATION OF A BODY OUT OF THE MATERIAL OF THE NEXT PLANE!!

This work is part of the Body of Light method that I have on my list of projection methods as method 3. This legend means that you can learn to make a "body" out of the material of the next plane, to which body you can learn to transfer your consciousness so that you can do many different things on the next plane by working in and thru this body. You can also learn to influence circumstances and events on the physical plane by working with this body from the Etheric-Astral planes. Not by direct action effect but in accordance with the laws of the physical plane, which is a course in itself.

So I trust you understand that if you *DID NOT KNOW SOME-THING* about the Occult you would not know what Paracelsus was talking about in the first place and you would either dismiss it as silly talk or attempt to create a man in a test tube as many have tried in past centuries and in either case get all goofed up about the Occult.

Question 5 — What results can I expect to achieve if I am successful in developing a degree of success in this projection Art? Answer — The very first thing you would acquire is a good sound basis of practical working Occult knowledge which is an achievement of no little consequence and should stand you in good stead for your other Occult work. The second thing you would acquire is that as you learn to project, and become more and more proficient in it, you should begin to acquire a knowledge of the inner planes that should help you to arrive at Illumination. How could you be associated with these things for a long time and not become better at understanding what the Occult is all about? Still another thing that you should get from this study is that you should definitely be able to find out more about the inner hidden side of things and first hand at that. This knowledge could not fail to help you thru this mad physical life so that you will be what is known as a Successful Person. Then, when people see you succeeding, they will enquire why, and when they find that you practice the Occult Arts, and this is the reason for your success, they will want to know more about it, and will come to you in droves for help. And to help them you will be able to do more than just talk about abstract things. (Never offer Occult Knowledge or help to anyone unless they ask you specially for it. Until they recognize a need for it, it is useless to them and only results in trouble for them and for you. Until it works for you do not TALK about it to others. It will only sound silly if it has not worked for you so that they can see it themselves).

Another thing you should acquire is that you should be able to explore and map out the inner planes, or rather set up your own paths thru these inner planes as there is nothing there now. This physical world is the tail end of a number of other "worlds" as you know and the CAUSES OF THE END RESULTS on this plane are in those inner planes. When you know how to penetrate them and study the causes of coming events you can alter those events somewhat depending on your power to do so. These things are not trivial believe me and their acquirement will give you a sense of power and peace that will go a long way to make up for what you may have suffered in this past mixed-up life.

The most important thing, that can be achieved, is to learn, in a positive way, how to contact your Inner Powers, or Forces, or whatever name you feel like giving them and, which is still more important of all, learn how to *USE* your Inner Powers in a positive manner. You have them, you know, but as long as you do not use them, by being ignorant of them, they stand there, doing nothing to protect you, while you suffer the "slings and arrows of outrageous fortune"

You are incarnated in a physical body for the purpose of learning how to conquer matter — (thy kingdom come, thy will be done ON EARTH as it is in heaven) — and if you do not start to learn how to conquer matter you will have to come back time and time again, over and over, until you do learn this lesson to overcome the illusion of matter.

Actually you know all this unconsciously and instinctively, deep down inside of you, but there is so much confusion in this life about what our aims are really supposed to be, due to the petty distractions of everyday living, and a deep outer ignorance of fundamental facts about the occult significance of physical life, that it is very hard for the ordinary person, until he begins to study the occult, to find out what the exact goal of living should be, and to get some idea of what the exact process should be to achieve this goal.

A start has to be made somewhere to learn about the other bodies you possess, and to learn how to use them. To learn how to transfer your consciousness, from the physical body to these other bodies at will, is just about the best and most pleasant rewarding type of growth that you could find to advance along the path leading to Illumination. These powers can come only with use and not by talking about them.

22

For example to be more specific — can you set or lie down and bring up images of persons or things into your mind mirror? Can you see, perhaps dimly, these figures and shapes? Can you then use your will-imagination to move them about and place them in different positions and make them do different things? Everyone can do this to some extent. Do you know what these images really are? These images are Etheric-Astral matter images and you are seeing them with the third eye. The single eye mentioned in the bible.

As I said we all have this power, in some degree, and it only remains to give it careful attention to develop it and thus double your abilities and talents to be able to handle life's tough problems. Do you want to have less?

I do not mean to belabor the point of the conquering of matter but this is what we are here for and that is *all* we are here for. If you are not advanced enough to understand and accept this idea then I advise you to reexamine your motives for studying the Occult. Just why are you interested in this study? You are not going to conquer matter by allowing it to hurt you all the time. You are not going to conquer matter by fleeing back up the descending evolution path, like the Hindu's Yogis do, by trying to ignore matter, by going into trances, practicing Samadi and ignoring all the rest of India's miseries.

You are going to conquer matter only by facing it, studying it to find out its reasons for being, and LEARNING HOW TO MANIPULATE IT. There may be other ways of learning how to handle matter and thus arriving at Illumination but this way will do for most of us until a better way comes along!!!

Question 6 — When one has learned to project what can one expect to "see" over there? The answer to this question is — I, myself, am so curious that when I have successful projection I explore all over so hard that I often wake myself, up, if I am in the dream method. I have at times found that I could see the reflecting ether very well and I practiced going back along the reflecting Ether time track as well as forward. I have caught glimpses of cities 1000 years in the future and also as little as 20 years in the future. I was in such a free state that time that I deliberately went around looking for **calendars** and I found one in a store with the date 2000 something on it. I am working hard to develop this facility and I hope very much to be able to bring back some real knowledge sometime. I admit now that I am somewhat shaky on these trips and I can get easily rattled going thru one of these scenes as after all a thing like this is not too easy or simple a matter.

Other times I find that I can reach a plane where it is easy to manufacture thought forms for certain kinds of duties (there is a technique to this as they have to be made correctly and endowed with life and emotion and energy in a definite manner. They can then be directed to perform certain jobs. This is another course in its self. See last section.)

I have not done much work on the life after death question as I was always too interested in this physical incarnation work. I did discover that there are definite "entrance places" scattered over the first inner plane for those who have just died and the surroundings around them are very much like earth.

I would not plan on contacting your departed relatives on the next plane by the use of these projection methods I am teaching. It is not that you would be bared by entities there but the road there is beset with strange difficulties and things are much different on that plane than what the world thinks it is. It has something to do with the real separation that comes with death that makes your live projections act very strange in that plane-place. Until you understand fully the state the newly dead are in things are just much mixed up and is nothing like what the churches teach it is or even what the spiritualists have taught about it for so many years. The newly arrived dead are in a dream state and do not recognize you or their surroundings with any degree of accuracy. For example I did visit my Father one time. My Father has built for himself a duplicate of the same silly place he lived in on earth for so many years. The earth house-place has been torn down now for many years, as it was no good, but my Father still lives on in his Astral-matter duplicate and he wouldn't listen to me anymore now than he would then when he was alive. So there he will have to stay until he wakes up himself. I can do nothing for him. So for heaven's sake don't plan on using this Projection Art to contact those who have passed on as it just won't do you or them any good and your visit will be of no comfort to anybody.

So now we come to the end of the theory instructions and the end of the *questions and we can start on the actual projection* work.

PRACTICAL WORK

Our first instructions on the Art of Astral projection is the method known as the "little" method (my name for it). I discovered, and perfected, this method myself. This method is the best I have ever found for making a start in this Projection Art. This method has many things to recommend it. The main thing is that it is very safe. This method requires the student to be in control of his senses at all times so no negative conditions can develop. This method requires study and work on the inner side of things which study-knowledge is of great basic value in all occult work and your achievements in this line can be extended to many other branches of the occult as they are all connected together. On the other hand this system does not require too much knowledge to start to work on, and to use the system, and the work can be carried out with a minimum of study, in the beginning.

When you succeed, in some degree of projection work with this 'little' system, you can then do a great many more things along Occult lines (I cannot emphasize this too much) All the "little" work is on the Etheric Plane and from that plane you can influence others, and circumstances, very well. This power is a very great asset indeed. Other applications will occur to you and I can suggest many more when I am contacted later on.

And, best of all, successful work with this system gives practical experience to prepare the student for the work in the advanced systems. What a beginning student needs most of all in occult work is something safe and positive to work on, and with, to develop his inner tools and to gain valuable experience as to what to expect to "see" when he does project later on with the more advanced systems.

HERE ARE YOUR FIRST INSTRUCTIONS AND DIRECTIONS —

In this "little" system for your first projection work you are going to act-project in a rather natural way. You are not going to go thru walls or thru closed doors or things like that. You are not going to go too far from the body. Later on, as you develop in this work, you can do all those things, go as far as you please etc. but for the very first work you will keep it very much like physical movement. You are going to travel a preselected route there and back. You are going to pick out a route to follow and stick to that route until you master it. So the first thing to do is to select your "trip" route.

Look about your home. Pick out a spot to start from and a spot to go to. Say, for example, you decided to go from your bed room to the laundry room in the basement. Say the route lies along the hall, down the stairs, across the kitchen, down the basement stairs, across the basement to the laundry room and then back the same way.

Now that you have selected a route to follow for your projection the next thing to do is to get to know the route throughly physically. This means that you walk over the route many times looking at it and getting every detail of it in your mind-memory. Notice every little thing about it. Notice things that you never noticed before. If you want to succeed in this work you will not do this just once or twice but many times. You will memorize the whole area-route so that you can recall it to memory without difficulty. It will not hurt for you to draw a sketch of the route. It will not hurt for you to draw a diagram of the route. I cannot repeat this enough — do everything possible to fix the route in your memory.

Now in addition to the ordinary fixing of this route in your memory do the following — Select at least six points along the route that have some special outstanding characteristic about them, a characteristic that you can fix in your memory easily. These points can be a picture, a spot on the wall paper, a crack on the floor, a vase or anything like that. If you want to make the points stick still better you can make, or buy from me, some symbols which have occult significance and place those symbols at these points too. (Contact me about these symbols).

When you have selected your points, and have reinforced them, then set down opposite the first point and look at it steadily for 5 minutes the first day and increase this to 15 min. in about 10 days. Do this for each point in turn. That is do it for as long a time as is necessary for YOU to learn each point and to recall it to memory accurately.

Now for heaven's sake don't cut this work short. If you get impatient and try to start the projection working without memorizing these recall points enough you are not going to get results and then you will be disappointed and will get mad and blame me for the failure.

I am going to explain the idea behind these actions in order that you, and your subconsciousness, will accept them fully AND DO THEM FULLY. The reason for the repeated looking at selected points along a selected projection route is to fix firmly the points in your mind-memory. Why do this? Your memory is directly connected with the Inner Planes more so than it is connected with the physical plane. When you look at an object physically you are not looking at it with just the physical eye alone, you are also looking at it with the 'Etheric eye' and the 'Astral eye' and the 'Mental eye'. but as I said before your center of consciousness is in the physical body for the time being, and when you look at a physical object, with physical sight, with the idea of recalling it to memory you are stimulating the etheric-astral sight too. Keep this point in mind — when you use the physical body you are using the other bodies too.

I AM GOING TO SUM UP WHAT I TOLD YOU SO FAR.

1. For your first work in astral-projection you start by selecting a route that you will follow.

2. After selecting this route you go over it many times looking at everything along the route carefully and noting all the things that will help you to fix the details of the route in your memory-mind.

3. Pick out, set up, or arrange at least 6 "points" along this route that you can fix in your memory firmly in addition to the other natural points, or you can put the natural points together with the artifical points.

Now here is something else you can add to your work on the

above fixing of the route points firmly in your mind-memory. Up to now you have been using only one sense, the sense of sight, to do this fixing of these points in your memory. It is possible to use your other senses too. (You can do anything you can think of, in your special case, that will increase your perception of these points, use any special device that is good for you especially to fix these points).

I experimented with all the senses. I first experimented with the sense of smell. I put 6 different scents at the difference places along the route. I remember that I used Vanilla for the first point, Peppermint for another, Chanel #5 for another, Carnation for another, Rose for another Violet for the last.

This idea was very satisfactory. It got so that as I recalled the memory of the scent along with the visual memory of the particular point very accurately. Then I experimented with sounds. I took a music teachers pitch pipe and assigned a note to each point. It seems remarkable but in time I could recall the scent and 'hear' the sound in my imagination along with the visual image. However as all the senses are in the "other" bodies too it is not too strange that they can be developed too and in fact your successful transfer of your consciousness to the other bodies means that you will learn to use the other bodies as well as you now use the physical body.

I hadn't intended to bring this out so soon but this seems a good point to do it. You are going to do more than just project, you are going learn to 'live' in your other bodies, *consciously*. Remember there are two more senses that you will have to develop on the etheric plane too in order to function there right. The sense of taste and the sense of feel. However you can leave this for now as about the only sense you need for your projection work is the sense of sight and the use of the sense of hearing and smell to reinforce the sense of sight. I do trust tho that in the above few sentences you catch some idea of your future work along these lines and the main objective to be attained.

I hope that you see for now that in order to succeed in your first projection work you will do anything and everything necessary to reinforce your memory so that your recall of the route you have picked out is accurate and will give you positive results. There are still more things that you can do to reinforce your memory but I feel that you should have enough for now. If you run into a situation in which your projections do not succeed for heaven's sake contact me about it as in a big subject like this I cannot give positive fool proof directions in advance. I can help you if I know what is wrong so contact me fast if you can't make it work.

I regret that so much preliminary work is necessary for you to do but this Projection Art is a great work and it is well worth your time and much pains and money. When you acquire a degree of proficiency in this Art you will have a powerful Occult tool to help you thru life and it sure can smooth things out for you. For one thing success in this Art will encourage you to take up other Occult things and as you acquire more and more proficiency in these things you will find your path thru life becomming easier and easier especially so IF YOU LEARN TO CONTROL YOUR EMOTIONAL BODY AS YOU MUST SOONER OR LATER. It is not the mind that makes trouble in life but your emotions and FEELINGS.

It does seem as if I never will get started on the real work but I do want to say another word about thorough preparations. Please do all the things that I have outlined. In Magical work, dealing with the next planes, thorough preparation is the key to success. I have known people who started this work the same as you are doing and during the preparations and before they were half done with the preparations they began to Project! I am telling you a real Occult secret now. In any work you do of a magical nature IT IS DURING THE PREPARATIONS FOR THE WORK THAT THE WORK IS REALLY DONE. This is one absolutely true thing about Occult work, (and this probably influences life to a much greater extent than known). The reason for this is that everything on this plane is the reverse of the next plane above this one. ON THE ETHERIC PLANE WHEN A THING IS CREATED *IN THE FIRST* PLACE (see last section) THE MEANS OF ITS CREATION IS DONE *AFTER THE THING IS CREATED*, and comes into being automatically. I do not have to point out to you how different this is from the earth plane. This reverse creation is one of the Laws of the Inner Planes. Enough for now. The above information will stand much meditation and study on your part. *DO IT.*

When you are sure that you have all these preliminary things out of the way and have followed my directions as to preparations to the best of your ability you are then ready to start actual work.

You can do the following work the way you relax best. The natural way is, of course, lying down. I have found that it can be done sitting down, and some prefer it that way. I have done enough work to enable me to know that this projection can be made while you are awake and moving about!! This certainly opens up some new ideas as to how this system could be used. You might keep this in mind and when you are more advanced try it.

In my personal case I am free in the middle of the day and I find that I can project quite well during a mid-day nap. However not everybody can be free at that time so your projection period will be something that you will have to work out for yourself. If you have to do your work when there are other people about you must guard yourself as well as you can against interuptions. If you are interupted during one of your projections along your route, no matter how urgent it is, turn about and 'come' back to your body by means of your memory route and reenter the body correctly and slowly and then "wake" up and get up.

When you have assumed the position you are going to use for your work and are relaxed and ready to start work then start by re-calling, to your memory, the place-points that you have selected as your route "stops". If you followed my directions as best you could and have studied your point-route-stops - if you have placed an outstanding symbol object at each point and have reinforced this with a scent and a sound — You should be able to recall these points to memory quite easily. Recall to your memory the first point-spot. Look at this memory picture of the point for a time. Realize that you are now looking at the *Etheric Image* of this spot. *Realize that you are now projecting.* Then take each of the route-points in turn and project yourself to each of them one at a time to the end of your route. When you reach the end turn around and come back the same way. Travel this route in your memory for as long a time as it takes you to be able to travel it accurately and quickly and get the feel of this travel.

When you have done this operation for a long time and you are throughly familiar with it, you then add the following work — Start at the first place of your route, your bed or your chair — Image yourself raising out of bed, or your chair, and starting your route. At first YOU WILL SEEM TO BE LOOKING AT YOURSELF DOING THE ACTION. When you have done this for a while and you are familiar with yourself doing the actions AND FULLY REALIZE THAT IT IS YOU WHO ARE DOING THE ACTIONS *IN DUAL* — THEN MAKE THE ATTEMPT TO TRANSFER YOUR CONSCIOUSNESS, YOU, YOURSELF, TO THE IMAGE OF YOURSELF THAT YOU ARE WATCHING — Try to see thru the eyes of the image, feel it about you, feel yourself into it. The image is your etheric body and you are watching it thru the 'eyes' of the ASTRAL BODY — when you WORK on or SEE any part of yourself you are working or seeing thru the body 'above' that body. So in this case you are transfering down and not up.

Hold your consciousness into the Etheric Body and go on thru the route to the end and back keeping yourself in the image. See thru the eyes of the image and perform all the actions with the etheric counterparts of the physical body, the etheric arms and legs etc. Keep doing this until you are perfect at it.

ONE DAY THE TWO BODIES WILL FUSE INTO ONE BODY AND YOU WILL OPEN ANOTHER KIND OF AN EYE AND YOU WILL FIND THAT YOU ARE REALLY THERE IN THE ETHERIC BODY FOR REAL AT THE SAME TIME YOU WILL BE CONSCIOUS OF THE PHYSICAL BODY TOO AND YOU WILL KNOW THAT YOU ARE DUAL AND CAN AND DO FUNCTION IN BOTH BODIES AT ONCE.

Don't lose your head when this happens. By this time you should have had so much practice along these lines that you should feel no great surprise. Stay out as long as you feel like it but don't go too far away for this first time. When you are ready to return to your physical body go about it the same as you would physically, return to the body and WILL TO TRANSFER YOUR CONSCIOUSNESS TO THE BODY. And you will open your physical eyes and ask yourself "was it a dream?" And was it?

There are some other things that should be called to your attention now that you are going to study these things for real — It goes without saying that you must keep calm at all times and do not allow yourself to get excited over daily happenings. If you become excited and all nervous easily and allow these things to happen it will hold you back in your projection work. Many people do not succeed because of this reason alone. Excitement, loud noises and all kinds of disturbances just don't go with Occult work and certainly not with this kind of Occult work.

You really should not do this projection work when other people are about, especially if you are likely to meet them on your route. As you get more powerful in your projections the time can come when they will *SEE* you with their physical eyes and think they are seeing a ghost, and indeed they are, and scream bloodly murder! (Many of the ghosts that are seen are etheric projections). Try and use all the common sense you can about these things. Act with modesty and restraint, especially at first, AND DO NOT TALK ABOUT YOUR OCCULT WORK TO THOSE WHO KNOW NOTHING ABOUT IT AND ARE NOT INTERESTED IN IT.

The old books say that for this kind of work you should choose a sunny day or a calm night when there is no wind or other disturbances in nature going on. If there is a storm raging or excessively hot this will effect the Ether and the Etheric Plane and will have an effect on your projection. After you are stronger you can handle all this sort of thing but for the start you should take it easy and project only on favourable conditions.

Now here is another matter that is very important and please give it your most careful attention. There will be times when you cannot project at all!! There will be times when it will be moderately easy to project or moderately difficult to project. There will be times when it will be a cinch to project and, in fact, you might find yourself 'out' unconsciously.

These times are governed by the phases of the Moon and the transits of the minor planets. It is absolutely necessary that you should understand this. It is not so much the phases of the Moon, in a primary sense, but the effect of these phases on your personal self. In general certain phases of the Moon effect all projections except those of the most experienced and powerful operators. Then again your personal work is influenced more or less outside of these main influences by, let us say, your personal horoscope set up.

The only way to get this straightened out is to keep track of your work in a note book and record the good times and the bad times and to correlate them with Moon Sign references. In this way you will find out, in time, what you can do and when you can do it and when you cannot do it.

I have a very useful reference book here and a calander that goes with it. The passage of the Moon around the earth is clearly shown day by day as the Moon enters one sign after another. It is possible to check constantly which phase of the Moon is ruling as well as what sign the Moon is in. By constantly noting these changing phases, and the signs, and matching them against your projection experiences you will arrive at the best times for your work. This is the proper way to learn this Art. You can get both the book and calander thru me for $2 (1960) I assure you need them and, in addition, they possess much useful practical astrological information that is ready understandable.

Another very important matter is this — At first I used to allow the student to go along by himself on his own power as it were. I told him to report to me at stated intervals and also report any trouble he ran into and I trusted him to do this naturally. In actual practice it has turned out that many people got easily discouraged when something went wrong or it didn't work fast or they ran into something of a hold-up. They just dropped the work and said nothing about it and I was lucky if they didn't get mad at me to boot.

Therefore in order to help you succeed in this work (and not for the money involved) I want you keep a diary of your projection work. Put down each day what you did, the time spent on it, and the results obtained, even if you did nothing that day.

The first six weeks of your work you are to send me this diary every 2 weeks. If I find that you are doing all right then once a month. If I find you need more instructions I will give them to you. This is very important so if you want to succeed in this ART please start your diary and keep it up. Many people, until they have tangible evidence of the power of this work, are easily discouraged and it is those I want to help by watching their progress and how they are following my directions. See directions in last section for making arrangement, for this supervision.

I was going to include, originally, the following in this book — How to extend travel with this system — To go to other houses. — In the same town — In other towns and places. I was also going to include directions as to how to enter the Etheric plane (because this system is an etheric one) and to handle forces therein and available for use on the physical plane. I was also going to include exercises and other things for Etheric plane work.

Now, as I consider the preliminary work that the student has to do up to now, I feel that including this advanced material would only confuse the student as this work is definitely advanced work and should come only after he has achieved a large degree of perfection in the beginning work. He might try some of this advanced work before he is ready and be disappointed. (None of this work is dangerous). I have decided to defer any further instructions on advanced work on this system until I hear from you personally as to your progress in the beginning work and how deep your interest in this subject is.

Dream Method

In introducing this second section, although I have said it before many times, here it is again. Real Occult books containing real Occult knowledge are as scarce as hen's teeth. There is so much endless TALK and endless educational instructions of theory with very little or ABSOLUTELY NO PRACTICES. (In the future I hope to get together ALL the reliable Occult knowledge AND PRACTICES that are available now and get them to you in a modern form and without any restrictions, of any kind, as to their use.)

Also, as we said before, of all the subjects of the Occult there is no subject of greater interest to the sincere Occult student then that of Astral projection. And again there is no other occult subject on which there is less accurate information available. The few books that have been published consisted mostly of stories of people-persons who had achieved Astral projection, in some natural way, and then told WHAT THEY DID BUT NOT *HOW* THEY DID IT. Or how you can do it.

Oh there were all other kinds of Occult information available, and in some detail — You could easily find out how to conjure various demons and make them show you where treasure was hidden — this knowledge available from the 15th century etc. but to learn how to release your self from your physical body (?) and then get back again has always been a great mystery. Every real Occult student felt that it could be done, but how??? (The knowledge was available but it was held up by the secret societies heretofore mentioned).

Whatever one may think of Aleister Crowley he certainly did the Occult movement a great service when he gave out openly the Occult knowledge he had been given in the Rosicrucian Society he had joined and with which he had broken.

When this knowledge was examined it was found that much of it had been taken from material that had been printed for several hundred years already! but had disappeared from circulation due to obscure reasons.

This discovery stimulated the search and research of independent students along these lines and the results of their work was published immediately, and made available for use, and not tied up in some secret group and given out only for group reasons etc.

Among the early independent students in this field of Astral projection was a self-taught pioneer worker by the name of Mr. Oliver Fox.

In the early 1920's there appeared a book written by Mr. Fox called "Astral Projection". Apparently the book appeared in this one edition only and was not reprinted. It is now long out of print and copies are hard to come by.

In this book Mr. Fox teaches a system of Astral Projection which he calls the Dream Method of Astral Projection. Mr. Fox says that he discovered this system himself and experimented with it for a period of 30 years prior to the date of the publication of the book.

The basic idea of this Dream Method was that a person could, starting with a dream, learn how to "wake" in the midst of the dream and, from that point of awakening, start a train of Inner events that could lead to a type of Astral projection.

I, myself, am greatly indebted to Mr. Fox because this system was the very first I ever found of a do-it-your-self-nature. I followed Mr. Fox's system with great interest and great application about eight years ago and it was because of the information and knowledge that I secured of the Inner planes, by means of this system, that I was enabled to discover the "little system", that you have already studied, and to rediscover and renew the Body of Light method, which method will be the next to be studied by you. Also to rewrite and modernize the "Symbol method" system which you will find last given in this book.

Mr. Fox's method is entitled to a very definite place in the basic work of every sincere Occult student and great credit should be given to him for his courage in following up and publishing the results of his studies in those early days when all Occult matters were viewed with suspicion. I am, therefore, including Mr. Fox's Dream Method system in this book for your benefit.

Mr. Fox's system of Astral projection, and all the other systems of Astral projection, are more than just attempts to attain some spectacular developments along Occult lines; you are going to find out some REAL THINGS about our physical world that is going to enlighten you in a marvelous way. I will not elaborate on these things, not even in this book, except to tell you that there is MUCH MORE TO THIS PROJECTION MATTER THAN YOU SUSPECT. See last section.

Mr. Fox's original material took up a whole book but he treated a great many other matters which he explained in great detail. Such things as the POSSIBLE dangers (which never were there) of Astral projection. Many of the other things that he mentioned I have taken from this section and put into the next two systems as we know more about these details now-a-days than the pioneering Mr. Fox did.

There is another detail matter here that I would like to call to your attention a little more fully than I did before in your work on the "little system". "Before" the real Astral plane is reached there is definitely another plane that exists before the Astral plane. As you progress in your projection work you will find out more about this "first" plane, which is called the Etheric plane, as you know something about from your work on the "little system", and you will, in time, come to recognize the planes by the "scenery" that you are "viewing". What I would like to have you understand for now is that, almost without exception, when you make ANY projection you first "hit" the Etheric plane. Later it will be shown that there is a sort of automatic series of projections that take place once you have successfully made the original projection to the Inner planes. What I want you to remember now is that your first "arrival" on the Inner planes will very likely be the Etheric plane. Be prepared for this fact.

At this point I would like to digress for a moment and repeat that since Mr. Fox's day in the 1920's a great deal of work has been done on these Inner Planes and many interesting things have appeared to be true that were unthought of before. I want to tell you here about a great Occult secret that I have discovered by my own efforts coupled with a few hints given to me by a noted Psychic in one of his lectures. I am sure that the following is well known in the secret societies, but could not be given out before, and constitutes one of those "secrets" that was reserved for the elect.

I hereby call your attention to the following — (also you should discover it for yourself as you progress in this work) IT SEEMS TO BE TRUE THAT THERE IS ANOTHER LIFE "OVER THERE" *THAT YOU LIVE WHEN YOU SLEEP "HERE"*.

When I first discovered this I first thought that that life "over there" was automatic and that all persons lived it but I have since found that you have to develop this life "over there". That is you do have a "body" over there now, as you have some kind of an organization, called a body, on each of the planes, but to live this "over there" life you have to wake up to a large degree "there"; and organize this other body and organize this other life, for action and movement, before you can participate in the full benefits of that life "over there."

I will add a few more things about that life "over there" but I will not be able to go too much farther into it as it is a subject for advanced study, for which see the last section of this book.

For example, as you may have suspected, it appears that a great many things can be done "over there" that can effect "here". It is thus possible for a man to build a life "over there" that can influence "here" very strongly. That is many highly developed persons "here" do, unconsciously, (from their life memory standpoint "here") build up a life "over there" that greatly influences and helps this "here" life. I am convinced that all the great successes, of this physical life, have done this second life building; and it is this second life that gives them the drive and inspiration and power to carry on "here" etc.

This is all I am going to say at this time. It is obvious that before you can explore the tantalizing possibilities of this "second" life over there you must learn, and practice, all the preliminary work as given in this book; supplemented with the other lessons and practices as given out by the Gnostic Society of Self-Development; which lessons and practices are at your disposal and service. And this is just the start of your extra dividends from your work on Inner plane projections!

START OF INSTRUCTIONS —

The following instructions are divided into several parts — In the first part you are to learn how to remember your dreams. In the second part you are to learn how to recognize that you are dreaming. — In the third part you are to learn what you have to develop in order to know that you are dreaming. And in the last part you are to learn how to "wake" up in a dream and start a projection.

First instructions — How to remember your dreams. Many people think they do not dream because they do not remember their dreams. The facts seem to show that everyone dreams, even animals. Many of us have noted our dog lying asleep and moving one leg while emitting low noises suggestive of running after, or from, something. Our dreams are quickly forgotton because they are very lightly impressed on our memory due to the lack of critical observation, to be described in detail later. Critical Observation is the main factor in this work of recovering your dream memories.

When you first awake in the morning you will find that you have a reasonable amount of dream memory retained. Concentrate on this memory and follow it up as fast as you can. Write down key words and sentences to enable you to recall details later. After a short while, of this recording, you will find yourself remembering your dreams in detail and without much effort. Keep a record of your dreams, writing down as much detail as you possibly can. I, myself, find this boring but the quicker you keep these records the quicker can you learn this technique of dream recovery. The choice is up to you.

After you have a number of dreams written down go back over them and study them again throughly. You will notice a very strange thing — Notice how, during your dreams, you accepted the most outrageous events and situations as natural and *THOUGHT NOTHING OF IT*. What does this suggest to you if this is the first time you ever thought of it? OBVIOUSLY THERE IS SOMETHING IN YOUR DREAM LIFE THAT IS DIFFERENT FROM YOUR WAKING LIFE WHICH ALLOWS YOU TO

ACCEPT THE MOST OUTRAGEOUS THINGS AS PERFEC-
TLY NATURAL and does not cause you a quiver in your dream.
However for the time being do not concentrate on this fact but
concentrate on getting this material down on some kind of a record
so that you are aware of this strange thing — that you accept *anything*
in a dream as *NATURAL* when it is definitely not natural, for even
a dream!

Now comes the next step. Your previous work shows you that
you do dream and that you can remember the dreams very well.
Your growing awareness of your dreams can now be stepped up to
the point where you can recognize that you are dreaming.

As soon as you awake in the morning, or even during the night,
your dream memories should be right there. By stopping any further
awakening and reversing the trend of the awakening process you can
RETURN TO THE DREAM. That is you sort of can "dream" it
over again or continue the dream with more or less consciousness.
Do not attempt to do more than this for this period of the instructions.

The next step will be to watch your dreams in action. Strive
to keep on a line not awake and not asleep. Allow the dreams to flow
along as they will and make no attempt to do anything more *than to
just watch.*

Now comes the most important part of the whole work, and I
will go into some detail about the next part. I am going to give an
illustration of an ordinary type dream. Let us say that you are walking
down the street of a city in a dream. As you walk along you glance into
the street and you see a strange sight — You see a small automobile
to which are hitched 8 green horses! The 8 horses are drawing the
small automobile down the street at a lively clip. In your dream
you merely glance at this sight and then proceed to go on about your
dream business.

Now if you actually saw this sight on a street in your city while
awake you would be bound to take definite notice of it. Why is it
that you do not notice it in a dream? The obvious answer to this question is that you are not awake enough to arouse your sense of attention so that it grasps the situation enough to ACT on it. If you are

going to awake enough to deeply understand that this is a dream then you will wake up and no longer be dreaming. If you are going to sleep deeply enough so that you accept this strange sight as natural then you are sleep and dreaming and cannot make any further move of value to you in your study of this inner plane. So now we come to that facility which you must develop in order to "wake" in the dream and start a type of projection on the Inner planes. —

The particular facility that is required, to enable you to recognize any strange dream sight scene AND TO ACT ON IT, is a facility which is called the "Critical Facility". The word critical comes from a word that means judge and the basic meaning of the word judge is adjustment. When you judge a thing what do you really do? Basically you make adjustments, in your opinion, of details and about details of thing etc.

This CRITICAL FACILITY is closely allied to waking life. Your work is to bring this critical facility to bear on your inner dream life. You recall that we said previously that in Astral Projections you do not project anything but consciousness, your consciousness. By means of the directions to be given, and by your practicing them, you will, in time, learn to project a large degree of your consciousness to the inner planes and still remain asleep. (This is also connected very closely with what was said previously about developing another "body" on the inner planes but for now all you do is project a part of your consciousness). You might say, to describe it more easily, that you first get a hand hold on the inner plane and then pull the rest of yourself thru to there!!

Now how do you get this CRITICAL FACILITY to function on the Inner plane? Well at first thought it seems almost impossible to develop such an ephemeral thing so that it will work. However it will work. And the way to make it work is thru a combination of Will Power and Desire.

We are all more or less familiar with the strange ability we have of hearing a tune of new music and then find ourselves humming it in a few days. This is exactly the same process that will make the CRITICAL FACILITY A REALITY IN YOUR DREAM LIFE. Still another strange facility ability that we all have is that of reading a story, or seeing a moving picture, and then finding out the next day that we have dreamed about that story or picture. This carry-over is quite common.

This ability, combined with Desire, Will, will do the work. All you really have to do is to think and desire a great deal about developing the Critical Facility and you will find yourself using it in your dream life.

How does it work?

Let us go back to the original illustration, that of the 8 horses drawing a small automobile down a street of a city which you see in a dream. What would happen if you saw this in real life?

In real life you would stop and stare at the sight and many questions would run thru your mind like this — Is it an advertising stunt? Is the car broken down? If so then why in the world have 8 horses and why are the horses green? What is this all about?

As I said questions like this would run thru your mind until you were uncomfortable at having no answer. The same thing happens in a dream. When you have developed enough Critical Facility, The dream discomfort would grow and grow until you reached the point where you could stand it no longer. You will then either wake up OR YOUR CRITICAL FACILITY WILL BECOME STRONG ENOUGH TO TAKE OVER IN YOUR SLEEP. Then will happen a marvelous thing. IT WILL COME TO YOUR DREAM CON-SCIOUSNESS THAT YOU ARE DREAMING!!! This point will mark a great achievement advancement in your Occult projection work.

I have decided to call this state of not-awake-not-asleep, the NEITHER STATE, and will describe it more fully later.

There is another important thing that I want to call to your attention, a thing that you will experience more and more in your work on the inner planes. With the consciousness that you are dreaming will come another kind of consciousness — that of being DUAL. For the first time you will realize that there is — are TWO OF YOU. One YOU in the dream and one YOU at home in bed asleep!!! This is a sensation you will not forget!!

You may come up to the point of neither state consciousness

of dreaming, and of dualness, several times before you are strong enough to proceed with the dream but in time you will be able to "GO ON" like as follows—

With the knowledge that you are dreaming, AND KNOW IT, you proceed to disregard all the appearance of the dream and do anything that you feel like doing. Actually you are now in an etheric projection. You can now turn and walk away examining everything in the dream with a critical eye. If you want to you can start looking for the Silver Cord that is supposed to bind you to your body. The cord has no actual substance, it is just a sort of stream of consciousness a sensation flowing "back" to the body. You have to actually visualize it a bit in imagination in order to "see" it.

Most all the "things" about you will be counterparts of things now on earth. They will be rather mixed up tho because there is no time on the inner planes, as we know it, and "over there" things are there "all at once". That is you can see the thing when it is new and when it is falling to pieces of old age use and the sight of both new and old at once in one is very telling, to say the least.

I need not go too deeply into the operating techniques of existence — function on the etheric plane as you will learn them for yourself first hand. You are being born again, which is the true meaning of the words in the bible.

Do you remember how it was when you were a very little child? Do you remember say, the first time you saw a chair, for example? You didn't know what it was but you learned in time. That is the way it is here when you first enter these inner planes. You have to learn the ordinary things of that plane all over again. You have to grow up again on that plane. However one very important thing is in your favor, you do have more intelligence than you did as an earth-plane child so you can bring your intelligence quickly to your aid, and quickly learn the Inner plane workings and doings.

I would suggest to you that for the first few projections you concentrate on working your Etheric plane body. Do not attempt to explore the plane too fully at first. Stay "still" watching, studying, classifying, absorbing, experimenting carefully, and, in general, giving the same close attention to your new surroundings that you would if you were in a strange new country which, indeed, you are. I urge the above course of action on you very strongly. Your intelligent entrance to this first plane will determine your future success in entering the other planes; which are still more different than the etheric plane; not more difficult but more different.

The "trouble" you encounter and the dire things that old maid occultists warn you against, all the times in the past that you read about Astral projection, is really nothing but this DIFFERENCE that exists between the different planes and what happens when you try to act on the Inner planes the same way that you act on earth-physical.

Some old maid New Thought practioner got out there one time, by accident, and when she tried to come, she went, and it scared the wits out of her. So instead of trying to find out what was wrong she labeled it all hell and warned everyone to stay away. I want you to understand this fully so I will repeat it again — On the Inner planes you have to ACT in accordance with the laws that govern that plane which laws are different than the laws that govern the physical plane. And until you learn these laws, and MOVE by them, you are going to find yourself in a very peculiar position when you try to do something. When you do learn the laws, and act accordingly, all will be well.

Now comes another very important part of your instructions which again I have never heard of from any other teacher and which I am giving to you as my discovery. This information is as follows — It appears, as a sort of natural law on these inner planes, that once you have made a projection from the physical body to the etheric plane, and after you have been there for a "time", THERE IS A VERY STRONG TENDENCY TO CONTINUE TO PROJECT AGAIN AND THEN AGAIN TO THE NEXT INNER PLANE!!!

Here is another thing that has caused much trouble for would-be projectors. You all know that you have had dreams when everything seemed to be going along well. You were walking along in the dream and, all of a sudden, you found it more and more difficult to move about. You could not walk anymore. Your legs felt like lead. Then you might "see" something and try to run and in the ensuing struggle you will wake up etc.

What has happened is that you have had another projection, as it were, and have gone over into the lower Astral from the Etheric plane. At the point where the two planes come together the "scenery" is very similiar and you cannot tell easily by sight where the line is. The only way you can tell is by the change required in locomotion-movement. "Later" the "scenery" does change.

Mr. Fox, in his book, does not describe this automatic projection as such exactly. He does describe something like the following — He says that as you walk, run, and do other things in your dream-projection you get farther and farther away from your physical body. He said that as this happens you find it more and more difficult to move. He also describes the change in "scenery" (which should have told him what had happened) that comes as you go "away" from the physical body location. He also goes to some length to describe a thing he calls the Warning pain. He claimed that with this increase in distance there came a pain in the head that also increased with still more distance. Now I have never felt this warning pain. (If you do you had better contact me and I will get Mr. Fox's original instructions to you). Finally Mr. Fox says that the pain gets so bad that you bolt back to the physical body.

However none of these things will happen to you if you follow my instructions and go about the entrance to the inner planes carefully and learn how to act there. You should have had some of this experience in your work on the "little system".

As you make your FIRST ENTRANCE into these inner planes via this dream method a lot of very funny things happen, the reasons for which I will explain later. The actual change-birth-over-into-the-Etheric is often accompanied by the darndest collection of NOISES THAT YOU EVER HEARD!!!! Bangs. Thumps, Bumps, Rattles, Cracks, Voices calling out names, including your own, and even loud explosions. The queerest kind of noises that you ever heard in your whole life!!!

Even when you have been warned about this, and told to expect it and what to expect, these noises are going to scare you and maybe scare you good. The noises may come each time you go over during your first projections.

After you have heard these noises for several times they should die away, but first they may change character — your name being called softly, a gentle knock on the door of the room where you are projecting. Your dog barking or your cat mewing, your bird chirping persistently. These sounds will more or less continue in your work, and always be present, but you will cease to pay attention to them in tine. All the noise I have left now is a sort of gentle hiss in the background. The worst noise I ever had was one time when I was working the inner planes and there was a really loud explosion that made the whole house shake, or so I thought. I jumped up saying "My Heavens the water heater has exploded" but when I went to look there was nothing, all was quiet. This was the worst noise of all. After that the noises died away.

In order to assist you to understand the reason for these noises I will explain something about them. However remember that this book contains four systems of Astral Projection and I have found that I can take some of the things that Mr. Fox describes and put them in with the other systems in which place they can be handled better. Therefore I will not go into a long involved explanation about the why of these noises except to say that, as an occult student, you should know that the way you cognize the physical world is thru your five senses. That is you actually CREATE YOUR/THE PHYSICAL WORLD ABOUT YOU BY MEANS OF YOUR FIVE SENSES!!! (see other lessons and literature issued by the Gnostic Society of Self-Development)

I will not argue about this as you can find out for yourself as you enter these inner planes. That it will be necessary for you to carry your creative powers, the five senses with you, and TO TRANS-FER THEM ON THRU TO THE INNER PLANES TOO, as you project. You cannot function on the Inner planes fully until you have made this transfer.

Thus, you see, the first transfer you made was the sense of sight. The second transfer you made was the sense of feeling as you tried to walk/move about there. These two senses are very closely connected and your transfer of them did not create any attention from you other than the ordinary difficulties above mentioned. But, however, when you started to bring thru the sense of hearing the fun starts. The sense of hearing is a sense that you do not use too much, certainty not as much as you use seeing, feeling, and the impact of the inner plane on its transfer caused all the unusual noise yet it was not really noise in the true sense of the word but only a disturbance. Later on you will take the last two senses on thru into the inner plane. I found I had no trouble with the sense of smell and the sense of taste. You will recall that I discussed some of this in the "little system" and showed you how to use the senses in setting up your stations along your route. If you did your work there you should have no trouble with this advanced work.

Now that the information about the noises has been given to you so you know what to expect along that line I want to return to the point where you were instructed about the series of automatic projections that seem to take place after you once have entered the inner planes successfully.

You recall I said that many dreams start out nicely and then run into trouble. At first you seem to be able to walk about easily and somewhat naturally and then there comes a change and your limbs seem like lead. This change in feeling is characteristic of the change that takes place when you go over the line from the Etheric plane to the Lower Astral plane. This change is the first sign you will have that you have gone over the line as I said before that the lower Astral plane and the Etheric plane are very similiar LOOKING. I am repeating some of this as I want you to grasp it fully.

Let us now assume that in your Neither State projection you have reached this point, where you cannot walk anymore, and with your Critical Facility aroused so that you note it. You can say to yourself "Oh! I must be over the line." You then stop trying to walk, remain still for a time, and then attempt to GLIDE-FLY!!! Restrain all efforts to move limbs or muscles. Will yourself off the "ground" and then will yourself forward or in any direction you want to go. You will soon get the knack of this.

I, myself, when I reach the change-over-point begin to make jumps, first short then long jumps. Usually about this time my Critical Facility is fully aroused and I take off. I love to do this and often do

47

it rather than do the more serious work of exploring the inner planes, that I should do, and get the information back to you.

I will admit that at times I have the fear of falling but usually the Critical Facility will tell me that there is no law of gravity on the inner planes so I let myself fall and end up with a good sound smack! but I am unhurt of course.

I will now go into a few more details about moving about on the Astral plane. However your work upon entering these planes for a long time should be merely exploratory. You are not going to do too much thru this Dream Method anyhow. Most of your real inner plane work will be done with the Body of Light method the study of which comes next.

As I said to you before the Dream Method is a sort of automatic projection method that comes into action automatically as you dream in sleep. This system is very valuable but it lacks the personal-direction-ability that is developed in the other methods in which methods you start from awake and go to the Neither State instead of going to sleep and coming back to the Neither State as you do in this Dream Method. However you should have this Dream Method in your development and so here it is.

As you move about the Lower Astral plane you might find yourself before a building of some kind. If you desire to enter this building you will, at first, go thru doors and windows. Later as you become more experienced you will go thru walls and thru closed doors. At times I have gone thru walls easily and other times bounced off depending upon the degree of Critical Facility that I had at the time. There is a strange sensation as you go thru a wall. A sort of drawing out and pulling thru feeling. I enjoy it very much and so will you when you get used to it.

As you explore about remember that there is a tendency to "advance" along the Lower Astral into the Higher Astral and so you may find yourself coming to a place where Astral matter begins to disappear and lights *of* colors begin to take its place. I advise you to stop there. You can do this by your Will plus your Critical Facility. Stop and return to the Lower Astral regions as your exploration of the higher planes should be done by means of the other systems in this book rather than this Dream Method.

One more thing and then I will close this section — Make a point, as soon as you can, of stopping and examining the "matter" of whatever place you happen to find yourself. You should find it composed of many thousands of fine points of lights and it should be moving about gently and have a sort of pulsation that should be quite noticeable.

Study this all the time proceed cautiously at all times and use common sense always.

While it is true that the material originally given out about this system took up a whole book I have given you the gist of it in this section. All you need to know to practice it is given here.

Body of Light Method

This section contains all the knowledge you need in the way of theory-practice to enable you to conduct a magical operation, for your benefit, called "The Creation of a Body of Light".

The name of this Operation-Creation of a Body of Light- means that you, by following the procedures herein outlined, can create, on the Inner planes, a body-vehicle that you can use for Astral projection and for many other things, and in many other ways for Inner plane work.

This "Body of Light" Creation is, basically, an extension of you!

In this section, and the other sections, and in this book, I am giving you some very profound Occult knowledge and practices. You must have noticed, by now, that this is no ordinary Occult book of the usual run of the mill stuff consisting of endless chatter about the dangers of using Occult powers for your benefit etc. etc. No, this is a book that tells you what is what and then tells you how to go and DO IT.

You are being given this knowledge, by the direction of Inner Powers, because the time has come when countless numbers of people are ready to learn, and use, these higher powers. And they are given now for the reason that you are to learn to use them FOR YOUR PERSONAL BENEFIT — to uplift yourself — to build yourself-up— To enable you to live your life BETTER, BETTER, BETTER.

It has been said before, and I will repeat it again, and again, the outer physical plane is the result of INNER PLANE activities. You cannot be successful in handling the outer plane until you begin to master the Inner planes (the reason being that each lower plane is negative to the plane above it)

It will stand to reason then the only way to influence this outer

51

physical plane is to "work" on it from the Inner.

Now don't go off thinking that this is something new, and startlingly different, presented for the first time. While it is true that this is the first time (that I know of) that these directions have been presented in exactly this way and for this purpose, to help you help yourself, this knowledge is not NEW. Every single thing that has ever been done on this earth plane has been done thru first working on the Inner planes. THIS INNER-OUTER WORK-ACTION HOWEVER IS ABSOLUTELY UNKNOWN TO THE GREATEST MAJORITY OF PEOPLE ON THIS EARTH. YOU ARE NOW GOING TO LEARN HOW TO DO IT "ON PURPOSE" *AND WITH MORE POWER.*

Forty years ago, when I first "took up" the Occult, the first thing that attracted my attention was Astral Projection. All thru these 40 years I have given this subject my greatest attention. I first gathered all the information-data that I could about Astral Projection. After a great deal of study of this material I begin to see some method to it; and gradually evolved the four systems that you are being given, here, in this book. Systems that I have tested and found to work.

Further research has shown to me that these four systems are basic and are known to many people who, however, secured this knowledge from others, under pledge of secrecy, which pledge keeps them from teaching them freely to those who desire to learn this Art, or even using it for themselves.

However the main point here is that these four systems of projection are not just that — four systems of how to project yourself Astrally — they are much more, and again much more. These systems can be used for many other things than just to enter those Inner planes and explore them.

After you have mastered the systems given in this book, to the best of your ability to do so, you will find that you can enter the Inner planes with many different kinds of purposes in mind and carry out these purposes, with positive results. Results that will astound and delight you. (This has been said before but it will bear repeating and I will repeat it again).

However please bear in mind that this book is a beginning book, as it were, and you will not find very much in it about extended practices, just enough to give you an idea about extended practices, and to arouse your interest in them.

References will be made to advanced work in the last section of this book (as also said before) when you have mastered the work as given here we expect, by that time, to have material ready for you so that you can go as far and in as deep as you desire along these lines. So give this preliminary work you best attention and master it.

The name of this operation Creation of a Body of Light means that you will be shown how to construct an Inner plane vehicle-body which vehicle-body can be used, by you, to project Astrally and in many other ways.

This Inner plane body is naturally built up and/or constructed out of the "matter" of the Inner plane. The "matter" of the Inner plane glows with a light of its own and the deeper into the Inner plane one goes the brighter glows the Inner plane matter. This Inner plane matter seemed like stars to the early clairvoyants and they gave this plane its name - Astral Plane - or star (like) plane. Also the name clairvoyant came from this same source. The word clairvoyant means clair—light and voyant-seeing — light seeing, or seeing by the Inner plane light.

This Inner light effect holds throughout all the Inner planes. In the Etheric plane it is rather subdued and consists of hardly more than a glow.   It is in the Astral plane that it has the real star like quality of intense points of light. As one leaves the lower Astral and proceeds higher the light increases from small points to large points and when one leaves the Astral to enter the Mental plane everything becomes all light, all forms disappear in this blinding light of all colors.

Also all matter in the lower planes starting with the Etheric will have the appearance of moving or flowing slowly about. As you become more and more familiar with these Inner planes you will learn to "stop" now and again and examine the nearby matter carefully. The intensity of the light glow and its movement will show you where you "are".

It is important that you should learn the following ritual and master it completely. It looks very simple and sounds like nothing

53

but I have found that this simple looking thing is one of the most highest and most powerful rituals that a man can use. I know that when I first saw it, and used it, I didn't see anything much in it but I found later that it went right up to the very top of the powers that govern and rule this physical cosmos! I was ashamed that I had not recognized it sooner, and better, for what it is. So don't you make the same mistake I did.

Now learn the following material and learn it so well that you will be able to recite it without stopping to think what comes next. It sounds easy, and it is easy, but it is a bit complicated involving, as it does, some movements and word actions.

1. Touch the forehead and say ATOR (Thou Art)
2. Touch the lower breast and say MALKUTH (The Kingdom)
3. Touch the right shoulder and say VE-GEVURAH (and the power)
4. Touch the left shoulder and say VE-GEDULAH (and the Glory)
5. Clasping the hands and fingers together before the breast say LE-OLAHM (forever AMEN)
6. This cross exercise is the preamble of the next section which is as follows —— First do the Cross exercise then ——
7. Face East. Visualize a steel dagger in your right hand, *Trace a banishing Earth Star, called a pentagram then——
8. When you have completed the star stab it in the center with the dagger and say —— Y H V H (pronounced YOD-HEH-VAV-HEH)
9. Still holding out arm and dagger turn to the South. Trace another star in the same way and say A D N I (AH-DON-NAI)
10. Turn to the West and trace star and say A H I H (EH-HE-YEH)
11. Turn to the North and trace star and say A G L A (AH-GAL-LAH)
12. Return to the East. Extend arms in the form of a cross facing East and say ——

[* See Diagram A]

54

"Before me is Raphael." "Behind me is Gabriel," "On my right hand is Michael," "And on my left hand is Auriel."

"Before me flames the Pentagram and behind me shines the Six rayed Star."

13. Repeat the Cabalistic Cross.

Learn this exercise throughly. Later you will expand this exercise in several directions. Do not force your learning but take it easy. However do learn it so well that you can repeat it quickly without thinking of what is coming next and thus not hesitate while reciting it.

For the next part of your work with this Rubic-exercise do the following—Take a teaspoonful of Whiskey, Brandy, or Rubbing alcohol, if necessary, and place it on some fire proof material. Do this in a dark room or at night. (Don't waste the whiskey or burn the house down!)

Light the liquid and note carefully the *color* of the blue flame, and also how it *wavers* as it burns. Watch this flame, get the *color* in your mind. Practice recalling the color to mind by looking at it and then closing your eyes and recalling the color. Do this for as long as it is necessary for you to recall this color anytime you think of it. At other times you can practice with a piece of blue colored paper, if you can find a close match, but use the flame as much as is necessary until you get this down perfect, and can bring this wavering blue color to mind anytime or place you are.

During this time of learning the visualization of the blue flame you are to keep up the work on the Rubic-exercise. As you work, however, start to visualize the dagger outlined in blue flame and as you make the stars see them outlined in blue flame, also the circle, as you make it.

When your motion-Rubic-exercise is done you should be standing in the center of a blue flame circle with four blue flame stars at each quarter of the earth, that is one blue flaming star at each of the four cardinal direction points of the earth.

At times the work will proceed easily and visualization clear as a bell.

At other times the work will be hard to do and the visualization dull.

Note both of these times in your Moon Sign Book and see if you can find anything about these times that are similar.

Now here is a new addition to this exercise. After you have finished the work as above directed then, before ending with the cabalastic cross add the following exercise to your work.

You are facing the East. Say (later you will vibrate) this Name EURUS (E-U-RUS). Enlarge the blue flame star. Visualize a scene like this thru the star. A beautiful dawn. Pink to rosy clouds. The East is the quarter of Air whose Archangel is Raphael whom you have invoked now for some time. So FEEL AIR. Let this AIR wash over you. Let it pierce you through and through. IMAGINE AND FEEL a soft COOL morning breeze coming from the dawn clouds and passing over you. The name of this East wind is Eurus so name it and call it.

After a time finish with the East and, gently erasing it from your mind, turn to the South. Say NOTUS (NO-TUS). The south is the quarter of Fire so visualize the tropics. Feel it, warm to hot, visualize blue seas, white waves dashing on rocky coral reefs, palm trees swaying in the warm breeze. Feel the gentle heat coming from this quarter and let it warm you through and through. Finish and erase from your mind.

Turn West. Say ZEPHYRUS (ZE-PH-ER-US) The West is the quarter of Water so picture and feel gentle misty rain on your face. Visualize a waterfall with clouds of mist arising from it. The water, after coming over the fall, is coming towards you and you feel it flowing into your sphere. Feel wetness.

Now turn North. Say BOREAS (BOR-US) The North is the quarter of the element of earth. These quarters have no relation to the usual ideas of Air, Fire, Water, Earth, but are concerned only with the principles of them. Hence the quarter of Earth, North, is not the north pole of the earth but the North quarter of Earth. It is in the quarter of Earth that all the other forces end. In fact *all forces* end in Earth, and the North quarter. Hence Earth is the great end storehouse of ALL THINGS AND FORCES. You will find in Earth all the things you are looking for and all the things that you need to make you happy.

So therefore when you visualize the quarter of Earth you first visualize all the vast areas-fields of things that make up the food for people. Great fields of ripened grain and vast fields of ripened corn. Vast orchards of Fruit trees loaded with fruits of all kinds. Then visualize great herds of animals grazing on their foods, the green grasses. All is plenty and full of Peace. Beyond this fertile land stretch forests of trees that furnish the materials for our homes. Then beyond these forests rise mountain peaks. These mountains contain mines of metals that supply other of our needs. And on the tops of these mountains is ice and snow which gathers there and then melts and flows down to the plains thru streams and rivers to nourish and water the growing things below.

Train yourself to visualize and realize all this as you say the name of this North Wind Bor-us.

Turn to the east and close the exercise with the Cabalistic Cross.

To continue this exercise is the work of a lifetime. Every time you do this it should bring you closer to the Elemental forces from which all material things are created. (The word matter, material, all come from the same root as the word Mother, mater, comes from, one meaning of matter is "with one".) Occult students will know that in the Western set up system of the Gods, or any kind of a God system set up, there is always one top God, the female counterpart of which all things come from.

In our own western system we have an early God Saturn. Saturn is the first fully organized God that appears in the system. The Gods before Saturn were more or less disorganized forces, or rather unorganized forces Saturn's father was Uranus, which also means the vast sky, or space; Saturn displaced his father and become the ruler of all things (up to that time).

Note that each God had a wife. The wife, of a God, is not really a wife in the sense of the word but means the opposite counterpart of the male God. The opposite God — Goddess — of Saturn is better known as Isis.

Isis is the Great Goddess Mother and the Great Mother from

which comes all things.

I cannot go farther into this subject here. I put this material in here in order to give you some thing to meditate on in connection with the development of this projection system. But I trust that you are beginning to see that there is more to this book than just a system of Astral Projection.

I have given you the above section of the exercise called the Cabalistic Cross because later, when you start actual exercising of the Body of Light, you are to use this exercise for that purpose.

PRELIMINARY WORK ON THE ACTUAL CREATION OF THE BODY OF LIGHT FROM THE MATERIAL OF THE ASTRAL PLANE —

Your first exercise-work will be of a rather physical-material nature. That is it will appear to be. Actually any and all things that you do "down here", any physical action at all, is not limited to the physical plane but extends "up" and thru all the planes clear up to the very "top". You cannot do anything physical without doing something Etheric, Astral, Mental and Causal as well. You use all the planes all the time, at once, and the same time, everytime, you do something physical.

This should give you some hints about the regulation of your physical life. I have every reason to believe that those people who are not world successes in the fullest meaning of the word, that is physical world successes, are not employing the Inner Planes to the proper advantage. Many people are very rich on the Inner Planes and yet cannot transfer these riches to the physical plane!!!!

Now, of course, many people do not want to make this transfer and that is up to them. If they really do not want to do it because they have some other kind of wrong ideas about money, fame, etc. then they too are making a mistake that will have to be corrected sooner or later. If, however, the non-transfer is due to a break in their work, and understanding, then this is not good and the break should be repaired as quickly as possible. To what class do you belong?

To return to our work-exercises on the creation of a Body of Light.—

The first exercise you will do will develop your connection between you and your physical body. The second exercise will show you how to extend this connection to your whole body. The third exercise will show you how to actually make the connection between this new body connection and the first Inner body. Then will come exercises that will definitely connect up this series of bodies into ONE. You will then have your Body of Light.

First exercise — Start by looking at your right hand. Look at it as if you never saw it before. Hold your right hand up before you. Turn it both ways. Move all the parts of it every way they will go and note the actions carefully. Then, holding the palm up before you, move the thumb over the palm of the hand and SAY OUT LOUD — THUMB. Then bend the first finger down over the thumb-palm and say FIRST-FINGER. Then bend the second finger down over the palm and say SECOND-FINGER. Then bend the third finger down over the palm and say THIRD-FINGER. Then bend over the little finger and say LITTLE FINGER. Do this slowly and very carefully and watch-feel the actions-words HARD. Get into the FEELING OF THESE ACTIONS.

When you have finished the above cycle then reverse the process and, starting with the little finger raise the little finger and say LITTLE FINGER, and so on down to the thumb.

Do this exercise about four times the first day and later increase it to about 10 or 12 times during the day or whenever you think of it and can find the privacy necessary. Don't stew over the exercise but do it when you feel like it and do it easily and without pressure.

After some time has passed include your left hand in this exercise and increase the time on it until you are doing the exercise for about 25 times a day, or if you don't like to do it so much then pick out your own idea of the number of times you want to do it. The point is don't pressure and don't constantly look for results. Just do it naturally and easily.

Next extend this exercise to your legs. Starting with the right leg first and then the left leg and so on.

Next set down in a chair and bend forward and backward and sideways as far as you can, saying the appropriate words as you do the actions.

Sometime along in here you should be able to close your eyes and see an image of your "inner" hands doing the same movements as the physical hands. Your "inner" hands should appear as grey-white-shadow-transparent hands before your "inner" eye.

Now you can begin to experiment, but don't run ahead of these exercises, Close your eyes and see your "inner" hands. Work the outer physical hands in the folding finger exercise and "watch" the inner hands do the same action. After a time work the outer-inner together and then work the inner alone. However don't get in the habit of doing the inner alone for a long time to come, your development requires that the two should work together for a long time.

I would suggest that you take at least six months before you go on to the next following work. If you should start the next work prematurely, and it doesn't work out, then you would be disappointed and tend to stop your work. This work is very tough and hard but tremendously rewarding and you should not treat it like ordinary work.

At the end of the suggested period of time. You should be able to "see" another body before you when you close your physical eyes and open your "Inner" eyes. You should be able to see, starting with your physical hands first, a complete body before you. This body should move the same as your physical body moves and with the same motions. This body should be able to perform simple motions at your mental orders.

You have now done one, two, and three of the exercises outlined at the start of this work. Now comes the work to definitely train the Body of Light to perform more complex tasks. You will do this in the following way.

First perform the exercise of the Cabalistic Cross with the physical body. When the physical actions are completed then bring a chair into the center of the room in which you are working and seat yourself in this chair facing East.

AFTER A LITTLE TIME VISUALIZE THIS BODY OF LIGHT, THAT YOU HAVE CREATED, STANDING OUT IN FRONT OF YOU FACING EAST.

Remain seated quietly and make the Body of Light go thru the ritual of the Cabalistic Cross, while you watch it mentally.

Do this very carefully and have the body perform the ritual in all its details. (You can leave out the four winds part here for the time being)

Again there should be no hurry about this work. You should take all the time you need in order to fully develop the working of this Body of Light. The more time you spend on the preparations the better your later control will be.

When you are thru working the ritual withdraw the Body of Light back into yourself and keep it there. Do not allow yourself, at this early stage, to idly use it for anything else than the working of the ritual. Practice this working and practice the control of the Body after you are thru with the ritual.

YOUR NEXT STEP WORK CONSISTS OF TRANSFERING YOUR CONSCIOUSNESS TO THIS BODY OF LIGHT THAT YOU HAVE CREATED.

OR YOU CAN DEVELOP AND USE THIS BODY OF LIGHT AS A FAMILIAR FIRST, IF YOU SO DESIRE.

What is a Familiar?

A Familiar is an old time name for a sort of assistant-associate-extension of yourself which the Occultist, living in the medieval ages, was able to create, out of other planes material, using knowledge methods adapted from the system-knowledge of the Caballa system.

You have been given the system so far in this book. You have been given some knowledge which has never been given out before to the very best of my knowledge. I am giving it to you as I would like to have you understand that many-all operations of Inner plane magical operations are very closely connected and not far apart as one would think otherwise.

Naturally it goes without saying that the Roman Catholic Church, which was at the height of its power during the medieval ages, was very much against this sort of thing and did succeed in supressing and killing many of the people who knew about this sort of thing and/or driving them underground — also discrediting them by labeling them witches and warlocks, the witch being female and the warlock being male.

The cycle of cosmic world forces have again come around to the place where the power of the Church as been greatly curtailed and these workings of Inner plane knowledge, can be rediscovered and recovered, by those who are clairvoyant, from the great store house of Astral reflecting ether images. This is the knowledge that can be made available to you so you can help yourself to a better life for you on the physical plane.

This object, the creation of a better physical life for you on the physical plane, is the avowed object of all the instructions of the Gnostic Society of Self-Development and Self-knowledge and Self-Improvement.

Again, as at the start of this book, I want to assure those of you who have some doubts about this work that there is nothing harmful or dangerous in this work. Actually the KNOWLEDGE ITSELF IS OLD STUFF AND HAS BEEN USED AND PRACTICED FOR UNTOLD AGES.

With the idea of giving you a tool to help you live a more satisfactory physical life I am going to give you the following information about how to use your Body of Light as an extension, of yourself, to accomplish many different things; the extension being commonly called a Familiar. I will then give you a list of things that you can train your Familiar to do and be and, so that you won't forget its importance, I will repeat this list at the end of this section.

The Gnostic Society of Self-Development has two sets of instructions already prepared which instructions have been used and tested now for some time by the members of the Society. I call your attention to them and I suggest that you send for them, at this point of your development, and see how they appeal to you.

While these instructions do not mention a Familiar in particular you can readily understand, from the development you have reached by this time, how these instructions work. The two instructions are called "How to be a Power in your Job, Lodge, Town, Group, School, etc. and the instruction is signed Sorel. The other instruction is called "How to change your name to a Magical Form," and is signed Agiel.

The first instruction shows you how to go about contacting the counterpart of the above mentioned groups, or any other things like that, and then influencing them in any way that you want to. The second instruction shows you how to make up a magical image of your Name and to do work with it. You will readily understand how to link this instruction up with what you have learned up to now as the work is very similiar.

The successful use of these instructions will suggest many more uses to you and you can always contact me, while I live, and get more (written in 1960).

Up to this point in this work the knowledge and training that you have acquired in creating and developing your Body of Light plus the knowledge contained in the two above mentioned instructions should enable you to enter the inner planes, to enough degree, so as to influence circumstances-coming-events in your favor. Work of this sort never ends and you will have all eternity of perfect it.

I am going to give now a list of things that you will be able to do, with a little more practice, with your Light-Body-Familiar in its present state of development and they are as follows ——

1. As aforesaid you can use your Body of Light as an extension of yourself and, used this way, it becomes what is commonly known as a Familiar. This Familiar-Light-Body being made of the material of the Inner planes can enter those planes freely and effect the matter-material of those planes in any way that you direct it to do. You can start circumstances working the way you want them to work! This is a powerful tool that should stand you in good stead in this tough life.

2. You can use the Familiar as a watcher. You can send it to a place where it will watch and record what is going on and then "report" the information to you when you bring the Familiar back to you. (Requires some special knowledge)

3. You can use the Familiar as a guard. You can form the Familiar into the form of whatever animal you want too, or any other form for that matter, and set it to guard something. If it is attacked it will respond back with a fighting system that is used by the animal-type-form that you are using just as if it were real and it is "real".

4. I do not practice healing of the body as that is not my line of

work but I do know that the Body of Light-Familiar can be used as a healing agent somewhat in the following manner — Transfer to the Body of Light Form the particular illness that is troubling you. You then treat-handle this illness thru your power of imagination — you alter and change the out-pictured illness, that you see in your imagination, in to a pictured condition of health. You can do this for others easier than you can do it for yourself as a rule (this is true of all occult work), but it also requires a great deal of Occult experience and power-knowledge and this work should be undertaken only after this power-knowledge and experience have been acquired.

5. It is possible to rebuild, in your imagination, your Body of Light as you were when you were younger, or better than you were when you were younger, and by a system of transference change back your physical body into the image of the Body of Light; a sort of reverse process from your first building up process. This is a very important feature of this work but, again, it takes a great deal of advanced knowledge and training-developed-power.

6. All things have a counterpart on the Innerplanes. In fact the real thing is there and not here. You can go, in your Body of Light, to the "place" in the Inner planes where these counterparts are and THERE MERGE YOURSELF WITH THE COUNTERPART AND THUS CONTROL IT. This is the basis of the instruction referred to before under the heading of the instructions "How to become a power in your Job, Lodge, Town, Group, School etc, signed by Sorel.

7. You can invoke, in your imagination, an image of some particular God force that you want to help you and then MERGE YOUR BODY OF LIGHT WITH THIS GOD FORCE IMAGE !!!! TERRIFIC EXPERIENCE.

8. You can explore the Inner planes and meet that which passes for inhabitants thereon. This instruction is given in the next section.

In the above, and before this, I have used the terms Body of Light and Familiar interchangeably. In these cases there is no real difference. The main idea in the last few pages has been this—Develop

64

your Body of Light and start to get some use out of it. I am hoping that as you go along other ideas will occur to you for use of your Body of Light.

Now before we proceed with the further instructions on how to use your Body of Light for Astral projection I would like to close up this section with a recapitulation of what you have been given up to now. And also I will repeat some of the things again so that you will be sure to understand it completely and fully.

You were given instructions which instructions have enabled you to construct, out of the matter of the Inner planes material, a vehicle-body-organization. You were able to "see" this body in your imagination. You were able to move it about under your direction. You were able to see it moving in synchronization with your outer physical body that is. You were told that it could do certain jobs and do some of them on "its own". You were given some information on some lessons on how to do this. You were given hints that much greater things could be done with this body and were told where to obtain the information when you required it.

All the above pertained to the creation of this Body of Light and its use somewhat on its own power as it were. That is when you created this Body of Light you endowed it with your own life force and life power, and thus it is truly an extension of yourself.

This is really nothing unusual. Everybody does this all the time unconsciously only you have done it deliberately. When this kind of work is done unconsciously the object created is usually called a "Thought form". Thus created casually they quickly disintergate and do not last too long, barely long enough to do their job. However the work you have done has been deliberate and was done with intention and the form, thus created, can last for a long time.

When you are not using the Body of Light you must keep it inside your Aura. You do this by willing it that way.

The following belongs to the end of this book properly but I think I will give some of it here in order to emphasize it a little more. I am assuming that, having created this Body of Light, you are going to stay on the Occult path for the rest of your earth life. I will repeat again that there is no other way to learn to handle this earth life than to be able to enter the Inner planes and to handle circumstantial things before they can "come thru" and effect the physical plane-world about you and also effect your affairs. Believe me there is no other way to master this earth plane. I feel sure that all religions that did not teach this system have been wrong. However you do find some of it in all religions. All religions deal with things called miracles and claim that these miracles were caused by their God interfering with the natural order of things, for the benefit of some believer. I will not go farther into this here but you do some meditating on this subject. Think about what religions are.

When you finish this book you will have four systems at your disposal. Four systems by which you can enter these inner planes and accomplish works there that can influence the final workings out of final-physical-matter-effects. I hope you will use these systems to your advantage, in particular, and also don't forget to use them for the advantage of the whole world once in a while. Its all yours go — to it!

I would like to also repeat here again that before you take up these systems, in all seriousness, and decide to go on thru with them: make an effort to clear out all things in your life that might hinder you in carrying them out. If this is impossible then do the best you can about getting external matters in their proper place and keep them there. More will be said about this later and some other suggestions given.

We have finished now with the uses of the Body of Light for purposes of it acting as a Familiar. We will resume the instructions for using the Body of Light as a vehicle for Astral Projection. I felt that I should give you all the information possible about the use of the Body of Light for the other purposes and also I did this to instruct you that many Occult operations are of many purposes instead of limited to one single thing, and some of these purposes cross over one into the other. Meditate on this.

I am going to mention another matter here and I will enlarge on it more fully in the last section. For now I am going to say only — in coming "down" from "no-thing" to something, or coming into physical existence from no-physical-existence, YOU, the divine spark, gained A DIFFERENT SENSE FOR EACH PLANE YOU ADD TO YOUR OUTWARD EXPRESSION. Meditate on this for the time

66

being.

So therefore in going "back up" to the Inner planes you really should "drop" a sense for each Inner plane that you re-enter. That is you really should according to the way you "came down". And when you enter these planes unconsciously in your dreams, or other ways, there is much confusion due to this lack of one or more of the senses. And this confusion is one of the things that seem so mysterous on these Inner plane journeys.

In the next step you are going to unite your consciousness with that consciousness of the Body of Light that you have created. Basically it consists of transfering your senses to that Body, and then functioning in and thru those senses on the Inner planes, where that Body is.

Now you did some of this work before so this should not be so new to you and if you did your work right in the "little" system you should have no trouble in doing it here. Also you did some of this work in the Dream Method only in the case of the Dream Method this transfer was somewhat automatic and in not too efficient a manner. However you should have had some definate experience in this transfer of these senses and the next work should be merely an extension of this transfer ability pushed farther along.

At this point of the resumption of these instructions the "appearance" of your Body of Light should be that of a duplicate of your physical body. Naturally you will say, "what else?"

It is true that for many purposes you will hold the Body of Light in the shape of your physical body. For healing as I told you before. And for making it take the other shapes for the other purposes as also aforesaid. But for general projection work and for the transfer of your senses-consciousness to this body you DO NOT NEED A HUMAN BODY SHAPE AT ALL.

Remember that you are learning a new Art of Living here. You are being reborn, (that is the meaning of those words in the bible) You are reversing the process by which you "came down" and you are now "going back up" and you are going to do this by your OWN DEVELOPMENT EFFORTS. Therefore you are going to have certain freedoms that you did not know about before. Freedoms which you did not have on the physical plane.

We can take some hints here from those writers on Scientific Fiction. These writers often project their stories into a future time when much of the physical work is done by robots. A robot, as you know, is a sort of machine man with a kind of a brain that works along certain lines and is of great help to people in that it can do many kinds of work.

In the early stories of these machine robots they were manufactured in the form, the actual form, of a man. That is with arms and legs and fingers and all the actual shaped parts that a human body had. The writers soon discovered that the robots did not have to have this human shape but they could be made in all sorts of shapes to do specialized work as required. For example if a robot had to do a job that required only looking and no walking then it would be made to rest on a table and equipped with multiple sets of eyes etc. Do you understand this?

The Body of Light that you have created is a sort of Robot in a sense. You can make it assume any form that you wish. The material of which it is created is plastic and will assume any form that you impress it to take.

You can, therefore, make use of this fact in transfering your senses to your (robot) Body of Light. You do not, therefore, have to create a eye structure of any kind, or even the suggestion of one. But you can if you want to. That is an Astral body does not need eyes to "see" with on the Astral plane. To see there you do not use any kind of an eye-type structure; but, to help you make the transfer, it might be all right to "put" eyes on and in the head of your manlike form of the Body of Light and then appear to use these eyes at first when you make your first efforts to transfer the sense of sight to this Inner plane body.

You will have to do this only for a time however. As you gain more experience in this work you will gradually discard this imaginary eye structure and "see" with the whole "body", at once all over.

The same is true of all the other senses and their functioning on the Inner planes. In learning to feel you will probably use, at first, an imaginary hand. And "feel" with that. Or you could say, to make it simple, that, on the Inner Planes, all the senses merge into one sense only and that is all you need on the Inner planes. As you now understand this we can proceed. Always start this work by doing the Cabalistic cross work with the circle in blue flames. Get into this habit. Especially at first.

Seat yourself in the center of this circle in a comfortable chair facing East. Bring your Body of Light in front of you. Face it away from you. Visualize yourself moving across the space to the body and entering it. That is putting your self *inside* the shadowy Light body. MAKE AN ATTEMPT TO SEE ABOUT YOU.

I just cannot describe the following process too closely. It defies description and I just don't have words to do it properly. When you try it you will know what it is like. The effort to "see" thru the Light body will work, if you persist in putting yourself into this body and making the attempt *IT WILL WORK.*

You must remember the idea of being born again and stick to that idea. Can you remember how it was when you were a body just born? and trying to see, move about, etc? Well that is exactly where you are now with this Inner plane body. Also do remember that there is really nothing-something for you to see there. YOU HAVE TO COGNIZE THIS SOMETHING THAT I SPOKE ABOUT BEFORE AND THEN RECREATE IT IN THE TERMS OF THIS INNER PLANE WHERE LAWS ARE DIFFERENT THAN THE PHYSICAL PLANE THAT YOU JUST CAME FROM. So you will not only be learning how to "see-create" on the Inner but you will be learning the laws of that plane, which laws are different than here.

Much of this has been explained before and you should have done some of this work as aforesaid. You should not have too much trouble. I will be available for advice but try to follow the directions yourself at first.

I rather regret that I have to mention so many of these "side points" all the time and I suppose that the critics will say something about it but I am writing this for you and not for the critics, that is I am writing it for you to learn from and about and that is not so easy in this kind of work-instructions. After all this kind of work is a tremendous thing. You are starting to reverse "the fall of man into matter" of which I will have more to say later.

To return to the instructions — You are now engaged in trying to "see" on the Inner Plane and "see" with a different "eye" through another different kind of body — an inner plane body and Inner plane "eye" (I am going to leave out of consideration here WHAT it is that you are trying to see. Actually you are seeing YOUR OWN CREATION!! In fact, as said before, the whole world is your own creation and so are the "things" on the Inner planes your own creation.)

Persist in holding "yourself" inside the Body of Light and pressure yourself to "see". Will that you should see about you. It is this pressure of your Will that will accomplish the connection in course of time; and when the merging comes you will recognize it for what it is. Practice, Practice, Practice, continually. Remember that you will have to practice this connection almost as much as you did when you were first born on this earth. A baby cannot focus its eyes very well, thus it does not see very well at first and it is a long time before it can distinguish between objects far away and objects close. A baby will reach for the Moon I am told and not understand when he cannot get it. You will have the same thing happen to you again here.

Actually the "place" you are is the Etheric plane when you first "see" things thru the "eyes" of the Body of Light.

You should be rather familiar with this plane and its laws and scenery as you should have done work on the "little system" and on the Dream Method system by now. The only thing that should be different is that you can now move about with a definite other body made of the same type of matter-material as the plane its self. This functioning in this kind of a body will give you a new sensation of power that is very gratifying.

After you have attained some degree of seeing and some degree of moving about, the next sense you will develop is that of Feeling.

The learning to move about is a sort of feeling but you can learn how to develop this to a much larger degree, and it will be necessary for you to develop this to a much larger degree if you are going to really function on these inner planes. By function I mean accomplish actions that result in effects, which effects are transfered to the physical plane. However in this book I will not go too much into this phase of the subject as this book is a beginning type; that is you first have to learn How to function before you can function in many different ways. Those who are interested, and I hope there will be many of them, can contact me later for advanced instructions.

As you will be on the Etheric plane, or very close to the border line of the Lower Astral, you can select an appropriate object on which to practice your Body of Light sense of touch-feeling. The "things" you see on the Etheric plane should be counterparts of things that now exist on the physical plane. Do not, however, select a counterpart of a living "thing". Influencing live things-counterparts belongs to advanced work again. Select a counterpart of some simple object, such as a chair or a table, for your first feeling work. Place the Body of Light, with you in it, in front of the object you have selected.

You can now extend a "hand" from the Body of Light and touch the object. The contact should bring a sensation and, of course, this sensation is different from that of a physical contact with the physical body. Again you have to practice and practice again and again this etheric contact. Run your hand over the object and try to assemble the feelings into something like recognition of some kind of form and shape. You will find that you have to create this form and add substance to it yourself as was explained before but for now just get as much ordinary feeling-sense out of the contact as you can. Your feeling will never be as perfect as physical feeling is so don't expect too much from this but on the other hand you do not have to use the force-feeling on the Inner planes that you do on the outer physical to accomplish results.

You will at first, as I said, extend an Etheric arm and do the feeling a great deal like the way you do on the physical plane. Later you will find that you can feel with the whole body at once and have no need to extend a hand-like-thing. You will learn to flow around the object and feel it that way. Still later you will find that you will feel by, not only "feeling" the outside of the object, flowing thru the object! You will find that on the Inner planes two objects can occupy the same space at the same time. If you would care to do some meditating then think what the reason for this can be. I would like for you to find out about the "density" of the matter on the Inner planes for yourself. Also remember that part of the recording of sense reactions on the physical plane is due to the use of your imagination also. You will learn that on the recording of inner plane sensations the imagination will be a much more potent force to be reckoned with. In fact later when you learn to make extreme journeys into the deeper inner planes you will have to look out for your imagination as in those deeper planes the imagination is very powerful and the "matter" of those planes extremely fluid so much so that you can form this Inner plane matter very easily into whatever thing you are imagining at the time and it will take that form and even say (Mean) what you WANT TO HEAR. Many people have deceived themselves in this way and imagined that they were Gods or were special messengers of the Gods etc. and made no end of trouble for themselves and for others who believed them. There are ways of doing this sort of thing right and I want you to do it right from the beginning.

The next three senses should be developed in the following order — Tasting, smelling and hearing.

Tasting and smelling can be developed the same way as you developed the sense of feeling. By this time you well know that you do not have to have a tongue or a nose to taste or to smell with. You select the object to be tasted and to be smelled and you flow the Body of Light around them and proceed to smell and taste and with the usual application of your imagination. You will not use these senses too much on the Inner planes but you should develop them to the best of your ability. Actually you will use the senses of seeing and feeling more than any of the others. The treatment of the sense of Hearing will be handled on personal contact with me. This sense is not like the others.

I have now given you about all the basic knowledge and instructions necessary for your to create your own Body of Light and to use it for certain functions. The work is not easy but it is not hard. Unlike most any other kinds of work and/or training this work is very personal and also very much of a concentrated action type of which you are the center and driving force.

If you will study the knowledge and do the training you will succeed in the degree that you are capable of doing so and, even in the least adaptable, of you that should be considerable.

I hope it came to your attention as you went along with the work how the different systems the "little system", the dream method, blended into each other and reinforced each other. Many of the things that you learned in the "little" system was renewed in the two later systems, and in greater force and detail.

In closing this section I will again recapitulate the work you do in this Body of Light section——

In this operation treated in this section called the Creation of a Body of Light — You create an organized center on the Inner planes out of the material of those planes. This organized center is also called a "body" but you found that, for all purposes, it was not necessary to have the actual form of a physical body but the "body" could be formless or take any form that you desire it to take.

After the formation of this center you learned how to transfer your center of consciousness to this body and how to function in it.

You were taught to function in this body by transfering to it the use of the five senses each in turn.

You were given a list of possible uses of this body after you had mastered its use and some of them were.

1. You can use the Body of Light as a Familiar. This Familiar is really nothing but an extension of yourself that will work and accomplish jobs on the Inner planes at your directions.

2. You can set up your Body of Light as a watcher and acting thus it can penetrate the Inner planes and bring you information.

3. It is possible to practice healing of the body by means of this Familiar. You can transfer the disease to the Body of Light and then treat it there and remove it.

4. You can invoke God forces into this body and then occupy the body yourself. A terrific experience!

5. You can cause your Body of Light to assume the form of

another and can cause an actual linkage thru which you can influence the other.

6. You can cause your Body of Light to influence the counterpart of a Firm, Community, Town. Society, Lodge, or any kind of organization that you wish to control or influence etc.

The above list does not complete the list of actions that you can do thru and with your Body of Light but should keep you busy for some time.

Symbol Method

And so now we come to the last method and the greatest of them all.

This method, that I am about to teach you, has been called the Tattwa method of Astral Projection or Astral Projection thru, and by means, of the Tattwa Symbols. This method has also been called Clairvoyance by means of the Tattwa symbols. In the case of the following instruction-practices the distinction between Clairvoyance and Astral Projection disappears and the two things become as one for all practical purposes; which is something I have called to your attention before.

I am here going to repeat the before mentioned Truth — the basic fact — that all outer things come from the Inner and also that the Inner is the Real "thing" while the outer is the symbol only of the Inner "THING". I WILL ALSO REPEAT UNTIL IT RUNS OUT OF YOUR EARS that WE (the fallen souls!) cannot deal, successfully, with this outer world in any way other than thru the Inner world first.

The above statement is one of the most profound truths in existance. As I said before I am sure that there is a race of people now on earth, and some of them were always on earth, that know this Truth and practice it themselves all the time. I am also sure that these people are self-born people, that they acquired the knowledge thru their own efforts and that they use this knowledge for their own benefits. It also seems that they do not want others to have this knowledge freely as they, apparantly, make no attempt to teach this knowledge to others. The few unsatisfactory conversations I have had with one of them, that I ran down myself, was to the effect that "when a person is ready the knowledge will come to them."

"there is a price that must be paid for this great knowledge and this price is that of refusing to believe the world and its appearances and to turn the back on all that one has ever believed in, or ever held dear — " "A struggle to overcome inertia, fear, and other hold-backs." "It would seem as if this knowledge was of such a quality that it must be gotten against, and in spite of, all ordinary manners of attaining knowledge." "this knowledge can develop ONLY against opposition — opposition is the food on which it feeds, the stimulator that creates." and so on.

I, frankly, do not know the exact reason why this knowledge is there and these people are there, and there is no attempt made to teach this knowledge for the benefit of the world.

I know that my own struggle was terrible. Fortunately I was in a kind of a daze all the time I was going thru the struggle. I lost every cent I had in the world. For fifteen years I was like in a desert. I did not come out of it until I begin to write these things down.

Therefore I do not know if you people will be able to make use of this knowledge or not. I do not know if any of you people will be able to understand this knowledge or not. To be able to use it without that struggle also.

A master did tell me once that the earth has entered the Aquarian age, some time ago, and it could be that this new age has decreed these things can now be known and practiced. In fact I was told that and I did write it down before but the signifiance escaped me until today.

So here is the knowledge. For God's sake take it and use it and benefit by it — as it seems that I can give it to you and, other than paying for this book, you have no other price to pay. USE IT!!

The instructions, to follow, will be divided into three parts. The first part will consist of the directions for making and coloring the symbol cards. The symbols you will use for this first work will consist of the Tattwa symbols. First the simple symbol of the element and then compounded symbols made up of combinations of the basic Five. The first coloring you will do will be the simple single color and then you will duplicate this in the complementary color.

And this instruction will be carried on in some detail in the last section.

The second part will consist of knowledge as to reasons for such and such a card as a certain symbol and why the symbol stands for the Inner "real thing".

The third part will consist of the use and practice of the Symbols — also their extension into other things.

Part One — The Symbols, their names, their appearances, how to make, how to color.

In this system, the Symbol Method system, you are going to practice Astral projection plus Clairvoyance thru a series of Symbols called the Tattwa Symbols.

The basic physical appearance of these symbols will be a diagram drawn and then colored, on, at first, a clean new sheet of paper-card board and, later, when you have mastered a little Art ability you will draw-color the Symbols on parchment and keep it wrapped in silk thereafter.

The appearance of the Symbols is as follows ——

1. Akasa-Ether Egg shaped, black or indigo also a shape called the Vesica Piscis which is usually colored indigo. The name vesica piscis is the name for the inside of a fish, cut open as it were. There is more to this shape than that but get it yourself thru your meditation.

   You will not use the Akasa symbol in your first work. So make the symbol for now but do not attempt to use it. Its use requires more advanced knowledge.

2. Vayu-air Circle — colored blue medium.

3. Tejas-fire Triangle — red.

4. Apas-water Crescent — white.

5. Prithivi-earth Oblong — yellow.

These symbols should be made on cards five inches by four inches.

In order to give you every assistance in making your set of symbols I will keep on hand here all the supplies that you will need to make up these symbols. I will endeavor to set up an address thru which I can always be contacted for some years.

The supplies you will need are —
1. A good ink and pencil compass.
2. The right size paper already cut to fit.
3. A good ruler.
4. India Ink
5. Good ink pens.
6. Genuine parchment. This can wait for some time.
7. Assorted colors of the right type.
8. Various sized brushes of good quality and a few other things.

I suggest that you draw, and color, a large number of symbols on paper in order to develop some art skill necessary to do a good job.

Also I suggest that after you have read this book, and studied it for sometime, and are ready for the Tattwa work you then contact me thru the address given, and enquire about the price list at that time. You can get, and accumulate your own supplies, if you live in. a large city where they can be obtained easily. Or if you have them on hand so much the better. Our only purpose in keeping these supplies, on hand, will be to help you, and to make it easy for you to make your symbols by keeping these different kinds of materials where they can be gotten easily when you are ready.

The first symbol you will make and use will be the Earth — Prithivi symbol. An oblong painted Golden Yellow.

An easy way to make this symbol is to set up your 4×5 card (keep it clean) Take your ruler and draw lightly with a hard pencil, two lines from each corner to the other crossing them of course, in the center.

Then take the ruler and measure $1\frac{1}{2}''$ away from the center cross on *each* line *away* from the center. Place a dot there at each point. Connect all these dots with a line. You should then have an oblong.

At first, unless you make the lines absolutely accurate, you will notice slight irregularities. Practice until you make the lines straight and the oblong perfect.

Now take the drawing pen and load it with ink and accurately outline the oblong. Allow the ink to dry throughly. When the lines are dry take your Golden Yellow water color and carefully paint the oblong bringing the color right up to the ink line with a small brush (in kit) Allow to dry etc. Before painting however remove the pencil lines from the drawing with an eraser.

Now proceed with the circle symbol. Make the same kind of lines, from corner to corner. Then take the compass and make a circle using the point where the lines cross as the center and using your judgement as to size. Then take the compass and turn it into the ink compass, ink it and cover the pencil circle with ink. When dry remove the pencil marks. Then paint the circle blue.

For the crescent and the triangle you will need some other kinds of lines. Now I am sure that there are other ways to make these symbols and a skilled draftsman could do it easily but I am writing this for ordinary people who are not skilled in this sort of work and do not do it for a living as it were. All these ordinary people will need are some simple fool proof directions. If you are skilled then make them anyway you please. The only point is — *you should do the work yourself* — otherwise I could furnish you with fine printed symbols much better than we can make but they would not have the value to you that your own work will have. In fact they will be useless.

Next you should make the triangle. Take your 4×5 card, divide it in half long ways, then divide it again in half middle short-ways. Now draw a line $\frac{1}{4}''$ of an inch below the short middle line. Then measure up from where this lower line crosses the middle dividing line on the long ways $2''$ and put a dot there. Then go back to the same point you started from and measure out on each side $1''$ and put a dot on each point. Fill in the lines with pencil and then ink them in carefully. Make them as accurate as you can. I found that I had to make several copies several times before I got one perfect. When the ink is dry paint the triangle in red color.

Now make the crescent. Divide the 4×5 card down the middle long ways. Measure down from the top of the card $1\frac{1}{4}''$ and make a dot there, call this dot #1. Now measure down $7/8''$ make a dot and number it #2. Now measure down again $\frac{1}{2}''$ and make a dot and label it dot #3. So you should have three dots numbered 1. 2. and 3.

Now take your compass, put the sharp point at dot #1 and the lead point part at dot #3 Make a half circle, it is not necessary to make a full circle. Now put the sharp point of the compass at the #2 dot and, not changing the setting of the compass, make another half circle, making the two ends of the circle meet. Where these two ends meet and cross should make a crescent.

Now change the compass to the ink pen and carefully ink in the crescent.

When the ink is dry the PAINT THE WHOLE CARD BLACK WITH THE INDIA INK LEAVING THE CRESCENT WHITE. Later on, if you wish, you can experiment with painting the crescent a pale lavender and also painting the card pale lavender with the crescent black. But for now leave the crescent white and the rest of the card black. Wash the India ink out carefully from the brush or the brush will be ruined.

You now have your four main symbols painted in their primary colors. It is true that there is another symbol called Akasha but as you will not use that symbol for some time I will leave the description as to how to make this symbol until the last section as said before.

In your future work you will need these symbols prepared in four different ways, or sixteen in all and, including the Akasha to be made, twenty all told. You now have one symbol made up and so draw and ink the outlines of three more of each symbol.

What you are going to do is to make up the combinations of colors and their complementary colors. The table of complementary colors is as follows ——

White —— complementary to Black and/or Grey.
Red —— " " Green.
Blue —— " " Orange.
Yellow —— " " Violet.
Olive —— " " Red-Orange.
Blue Green " " Russet.
Violet —— " " Citrine.
Reddish Orange " " Green Blue.
Deep Amber " " Indigo.
Lemon Yellow " " Red Violet.
Yellow Green " " Crimson.

You can now proceed to paint in the proper colors on the outlines that you have prepared. We will again start with the Earth symbol. You have now an Earth symbol — a square oblong — painted golden yellow. Take your next inked outline. Paint the square Golden Yellow. Then paint the remainder of the space on the card, around the symbol, Violet. Do a good job. Next take another inked symbol and reverse this color scheme. Paint the symbol violet and the background golden yellow. Take another inked symbol, paint the 'symbol Violet and leave the background white. You now have the Earth symbol in four different combinations and in later work you will use the different cards for different kinds of work, some of which will be explained in the last section.

Next take the symbol of Water, the crescent. This one is a little different because of the white and black and because the paper is already white which makes it a little confusing. The symbol you have now is a white crescent with a black background. (if you want to you can use white paint on this white part but white paint is a little funny to handle and really doesn't look very white.) However for these symbols you had better use the white paint and not depend on the white of the paper for your white symbol color. Putting the white paint on will at least give you the feel of doing something about it.

So take your inked crescent and paint the crescent black and leave the rest white or paint it white as aforesaid but there is so much space here that I will leave it up to you as to what you want to do. Take another inked symbol and paint the symbol white and leave the background white. I agree this is a little confusing but leave it that way for now and later you will understand it better. This confusion is typical of the element of Water and its inherent nature which nature is instability and changeableness in many degrees.

Next take the symbol of Fire the triangle. You have one in which the triangle is painted red and the background left white. Take an inked outline. Paint the triangle green and the background red. Take another inked outline. Paint the triangle red and then paint the background green. Take another inked outline. Paint the

81

triangle green and leave the background white.

Next take the symbol of Air the circle. You have one in which the circle is blue and the background is white. Take an inked outline of the circle. Paint the circle blue and the background orange. Take another inked outline. Paint the circle orange and the background blue. Take another inked outline. Paint the circle orange and leave the background white.

This should complete the work for the preliminary layout of your Elemental Symbols. I trust that you learned to enjoy this work. Making magical tools is a fascinating occupation. You are probably tired now and ready to take a rest from these labors but I hope I won't startle you by reminding you that you will have to do this all over again and on parchment. That is if you want to get the very best results from your work. But you won't have to do this for some time yet and you can learn all the operating techniques from these paper cards.

This is properly the end of section one. The reason for these symbols being the shapes they are and the connections thereby to the Inner forces they represent will be explained in part two, which follows.

I would like to call to your attention that, as far as I have been able to find out, no one else has ever taught that different kinds of symbols could be used and used for different kinds of things-operations. There has been some information given about the use of the simple symbol, the symbol with the inked outline painted in the primary color, but none about the other kinds of reversed colors, those that you have just painted. These symbols have reversed uses as for example if you are working for yourself you will use one kind of symbol and if you are working for others you will use another kind of symbol. If you are working for things in general you will use another kind of color arrangement. Some of these uses will be given to you and some you will have to get thru your own efforts. Several times here I have used different spellings for the Tattvas. I did this on purpose because different books and persons spell them differently and I want you to recognize the word no matter how it is spelled.

Part Two — The Why of a certain shape of a certain Symbo for a certain thing. (Never explained before to my knowledge)

The Word Symbol comes from two greek words which mean throw and together or throw together or put together as we might say. In the sense that we are using the word symbol in this book we mean in-place-of or a visible sign of something that is invisible. An outer sign symbol that will represent the force thing we deal with on the Inner plane.

You have probably noticed from time to time that occasionally a symbol will represent something to which the symbol apparantly has no relation and then others times symbols will have a very direct connection with the thing represented. For example, in the old days, an Inn was marked by a bunch of tree branches hanging from a pole thru an upper window. This symbol told the traveler in those days that the building was an Inn. There is a connection, no doubt, but as I don't know about it I would not recognize this building as an Inn. However if the building had a symbol on it of a large sign board with a picture of food painted on it I would recognize the connection easily and so can anyone else. Do some meditation on symbols yourself and see what you come up with.

Now in the present symbol matter that we are considering you have made four symbols on some cards and have painted them in certain colors. The symbols were as follows — A Blue Circle — A Red Triangle — a White Crescent. An Oblong Yellow Square.

You have been told that these symbols represent Air, Fire, Water, and Earth, and I will admit that, at first glance, it is hard to detect any connection between these symbols and the aforesaid Elements. You have been doing some work with these forces heretofor and, although I had not explained the matter fully and in detail, it was not really necessary for you to know fully about these forces in order to get results from working with them. Now, however, I will explain the elemental forces, and their symbols, fully and completely and again, as far as I am aware, this is the only time this exact knowledge-explanation has appeared in print. All the other writers have talked glibly about "forces" Elemental forces, Air, Fire, Water, Earth. etc.

etc. but what do they mean? Well they just don't explain what they mean and probably because they are fuzzy themselves about the real inner meaning of these things. Then again, as I also said before, they might be bared from revealing these things as they learned them under oaths of secrecy, and cannot tell them to others freely. Well what ever the reason is here it is now and learn it well. (The following information is worth the price of this book alone.)

The "things" called Air, Fire, Water, and Earth are not really Air, Fire, Water, and Earth of the physical type you, and everyone else, is familiar with. To understand them you will have to make a radical departure from your ordinary type of thinking, and begin to really "THINK".

"THE THINGS CALLED AIR, FIRE, WATER, AND EARTH ARE QUALITIES, QUALITIES, QUALITIES, AND NOT THINGS, PHYSICAL THINGS".

These QUALITIES are what make up the Physical Universe. Not the Inner Universe beyond the Mental plane, as was told previously, or, not beyond the point where THINGS become FORCES. Or, rather, were all things become one thing and all senses becomes one sense. Recall what I told you before — that as you came "down" the planes you gained another "sense" each plane you entered. Also recall I told you part of your work on illumination was to take the developed senses "back up" the Inner planes, and keep control of them instead of losing them, to a sort of half way place WHERE EARTH MEETS HEAVEN. Remember these things, and don't forget them.

So as these elemental forces are QUALITIES, what are qualities and what does this mean? Let us consider the element of Air. What would the quality of Air be? (The word quality comes from the Latin word qualitas which means how-constituted, and the word constituted comes from two Latin words con-stituere; con means with and stituere means place. Any help?) If there is one thing that could be said to be the quality of Air that one thing is Motion. Air is constantly in motion. Air means the gases also and those of you who have studied physics were taught that the molecules of all gases are trying to get as far away from each other as is possible. Movement. Motion.

84

The Ability to move. To be able to move. Moveableness. Can you see some connection between a circle and the quality of being able to move? Most all things that are round are movable. Look at wheels, gears. Anything that is round can be moved by pushing or rolling. However roundness still does not explain the exact connection between a circle, Air, and the moveableness that it represents. Here is the connection.

Certain systems and certain teachers have compared physical creation by the following SYMBOL ILLUSTRATION. The first manifestation to flow into the outer from the inner has be described as a single dot. DOT. Picture it.

This single dot is then described as moving out to form a line (line of dots). Picture a line. Now usually at this point they say the line of dots turns a 45 degree corner and then turns again and again and so back to the original starting point. Then lines drop down from the corners and turn again so that a square is formed.

This, however, is not the case at all. The above described symbol development would make no allowance for the other elements of expansion, contraction, and solidity, but would make the quality of movement the only element and, by the above symbol description, make movement-ableness go directly into solidity. The actual creation process consists of each element-quality coming into play in turn and matter, such as we know it, is the result. A result combining all the qualities in one. The exact physical creation process, as shown by a symbol process, is as follows. —

Let us consider the Dot as continued be-ing. Consider the dots so close together that they constitute a line continuous "And these dots are flowing into being continually." Thus the QUALITY OF MOVEABLENESS would go on forever if the next element-quality did not come into plan-play. (Each element-quality creates the conditions which lead to the next element's appearance.) (You will have to imagine too that each of these element-qualities have certain "built in" limitations which causes the element to reach an end to its activity and thus makes way for the next element to appear.)

To make this illustration easier for our physical mindness to understand, let us imagine that this continual inflow of dots, becomming lines, creates pressures (on its own type of plane) which pressure results in expansion- pressures that must be allowed to escape in some way, AND THE LINE OF DOTS, HAVING REACHED ITS LIMITS SIDEWAYS BEGANS TO EXPAND FROM THE MIDDLE OUTWARDS (see Akasa symbol). Although you have not made this symbol you can see it in the next section and you were told that it was Akasa (I did not give you directions for making this symbol as yet because I did not want any of you to use to use it even accidentally as it is rather difficult to use and different. Akasa is the first element and it is not so clear in its purpose as are the others and not so easily understood. Also there is no Archangel names to go with it and the names to be used have to come from some other sources of knowledge not readily available to you as a student.)

The line of dots then becomes the double convex symbol called Akasa and this figure, on further expansion, becomes the Air circle symbol.

I will repeat this as I want you to understand it fully. The element Akasa becomes the element Air and the symbol, the double convex figure expands out from in to become a circle as you can readily see.

As the element Air is formed it begins to manifest its quality of motion. Not only is its symbol a circle but it is also said to be circular in shape-form and as its quality is motion it has to move and the only way it can move is by turning around and around. And this it does, faster and faster.

This turning generates heat and this heat causes expansion the same as physical heat causes expansion. This generated heat is the pressure-force that causes the next element to come into being — the element of Fire. EXPANSION IS THE QUALITY OF FIRE.

The generated heat-expansion brings pressures on the circle and, due to the before mentioned limits of pressure, the circle begans to give way to another form and the element of Air begans to give way to another element, that of Fire. You will have to picture the circle being pushed out at three points and each of these points becomes the point of a triangle and thus the circle turns into a Fire triangle symbol. The quality of Fire is EXPANSION.

86

Now the triangle of Fire is allowed to expand only again so much due to the same forces that limited the other elements in their "size". The only way the Fire triangle can expand is along its base and as the base expands outward the upper point collapses down and the triangle becomes a crescent, THE CRESCENT OF WATER. Or it could be said that the over-expansion of the Fire triangle causes a contraction of the triangle INTO ANOTHER DIMENSION and this is true of each of these elements. Each of the changes is the result of the element passing on out into the next plane. Thus the symbol triangle of Fire becomes the Water crescent thru the force of contraction AND CONTRACTION IS THE QUALITY OF WATER.

The force of contraction continues its course and this force makes the crescent began to assume the oblong square shape of the element of EARTH. THE QUALITY OF THE ELEMENT OF EARTH IS STABILITY-INERITA —

The square-oblong symbol and the EARTH itself is the final result of the activity expressed in the Elemental forces from their start of their coming into "existance" and by "their" passage thru each of the elemental states, one into the other, and not by the line turning corners and ending up in a square as many of the old teachers and their schools taught.

Do you understand now some connection between the symbols and the Inner Thing they symbolize, the "real" thing. You can see that these symbols are not arbitrary figures but actual pictures of the real forces and the actual changes that the symbols go thru to change one into the other is the same change that the elemental force goes thru to change from one force into the others in turn.

Do meditation on this and keep it up until you understand it well.

And now we come to the third part of these instructions — The use and practice of these symbols and some ideas of their extension and application to other things.

The symbols you have been studying, and all other symbols, of all kinds, are connected with the "real" thing that they represent by definite bonds of a certain kind. In fact it is the basic teaching of

87

Occultism that if one goes deeply enough into the deep consciousness of us all all things become one. I mentioned something about this before when I told you that if and when you penetrated deeply enough into the planes you would find that all things become one. All senses become one sense, forms disappear into colors and these colors merge into white or black etc.

However for our purposes we are living on the outer physical plane and therefore all we see is the outer symbol. So that is what we have to work with, the outer symbol. As I said if you go deep enough all things become one, but long before that stage is reached there are other "connections" to the Inner thing from the outer symbol. Primitive peoples were more aware of these inner connections than we are. Primitive peoples brought on a type of clairvoyance by means of crude drugs from plants and other natural sources and were thereby able to "see" clairvoyantly these actual connections in the form of long lines of substance of the material of the etheric plane running between the outer symbol object and the disappearing into the Inner planes. Also they were able to see these connections, in the form of lines of light, connecting all objects that were related to each other, in any way, shape or form.

A great deal of this is told and explained in a book called "The Secret Science behind Miracles." by Max Freedom Long. Some work has been done along these lines by Mr. Long. I was in contact with him some years ago and he told me then that he was frankly experimenting and did not know too much about the exact powers that could be developed thru this study. As he was of no help to me I lost contact with him and went my own way. I am now more or less in a position to be able to set up a definate course of instructions based on this book. I believe I could now teach and train anyone with a small amount of psychic tendencies-powers to begin with, to become a fair Kahuna as the practitioners of this Art are called or were called, in the old time. You will find at the end of this book a list of Occult works which are those that I consider useful to the study of Occultism and these books are the best in the world for this study. And are just about the only ones that are worth a plugged nickel when it comes to good sound practical knowledge and practices.

More will be said about these books later but for now I am going to tell you that I will keep these books on hand in stock at all times and you can get them from me by contacting me. I am not doing this to make money off the sale of books but I know what a time I had to find good books during the years I was studying and I was very fortunate because for a time I had some money and some time to look for these books. Some of these books will be out of print but I will try to have them, in some form, for you.

So to get back to the symbols and their workings. You can take my word for it for now that the symbol of a thing is connected with the thing. Thus these symbols, and all symbols, are connected with the inner real things and thru this innate power connection you can connect-contact yourself, your personal self, your personality-powers, with the Inner things, and INFLUENCE THESE INNER THINGS AS YOU WILL OR WILL NOT. Also the symbols are doors thru which you can enter the inner planes, pass thru them, and then return to this plane with your knowledge.

However you have had some instruction on working with symbols for the attainment of certain physical ends elsewhere in this book and therefore I am going to devote this section to the Art of using the elemental symbols as doors to the Inner planes AND ALSO, BY THIS METHOD, TO COME INTO TOUCH WITH THE INHABITANTS OF THOSE INNER PLANES.

Not a great deal will be said in this book about the inhabitants of these Inner planes. This is a great and terrific subject and cannot be handled in this little book. Then again this is a beginner's book to start students out on this work. Some reference will be made to this subject later. The object of this book is to *START* you on the way to becomming a Master of the Art, and you will need more knowledge and technical information than I can give you while you are still learning the beginnings of this Art.

For the first Inner plane work of this system that I am now teaching you you should use the symbol of the element of Earth — the golden yellow oblong. (Later on you will learn about another form of this Earth element symbol which symbol is called Earth of Earth. In case you know about this symbol already I do not mean the Earth of Earth symbol but the ordinary golden oblong Earth symbol.)

First — Set up your room. For this work you can have a small table in the center of the room and a comfortable chair as well as a source of good light but not too bright.

First perform the cabalistic cross ritual. Always preceed your work with this ritual — do the four winds part also. When you have reached the forth quarter, have invoked the Archangel Auriel and visualized the scene described previously for this quarter, then, instead of proceeding with the ritual and closing it you can stop at this point. You may seat yourself and arrange the table and chair so that you face the quarter of the North. You should have on the table the card with the Golden Yellow oblong on it and also another card of the same size which should be blank white. You may also have a support to hold the card upright so that you don't have to hold it in your hand during this work.

When you are ready take up the symbol and gaze at it steadly for about two-three minutes. The light should be focused on the card but not be too bright. You may blink your eyes easily. Do not strain yourself but act naturally and relaxed. If you find you can hold the card steady then hold it but if you can't then use the stand.

After two or three minutes set the symbol card down and pick up the white blank card and gaze on it. You should see, outlined on the white card, the oblong symbol but in the complementary color which, in this case, is violet. The violet symbol will have a tendency to disappear and then appear for some time, before it fades away.

Now close your eyes. You will see the violet square before you by the reflex action of your sense of sight. Forcefully visualize this square and MAKE IT BECOME LARGE BEFORE YOU. That is enlarge it in your imagination until it becomes large enough to act LIKE A DOOR. *NOW, IN YOUR IMAGINATION, STEP THRU THIS DOOR. SEE AND FEEL YOURSELF GOING THRU THIS VIOLET SQUARE AS IF IT WAS A DOOR. SENSE AND FEEL THE DOOR CLOSING BEHIND YOU.* MAKE AN EFFORT TO FEEL YOURSELF INSIDE THE ELEMENT OF EARTH.

You should have visualized this scenery of this North quarter many times before this. NOW YOU ARE THERE INSIDE IT!!! Make an effort to see about you. Make an effort to SEE the scene that you have visualized so many times before. (Note — Your work on the Body of Light method should have prepared you for this experience very well. In fact you will probably be functioning in the Body of Light as you go thru this door the first time. This can be automatic. In the original work as given in the sources from which this was taken there was no previous work on different systems at all. In this book you are given an advantage that previous students never had. They started the work with the symbol method with no previous experience on the inner planes. By now you have had a great deal of this work-experience and this should help you greatly).

After you have entered the door several times and have made several attempts to look about you and when you have gotten some feel of the element and of being inside it you can proceed to sound off, or vibrate, the following names — Vibrate aloud the divine name Adonai-ha-aretz — three or four times. Then vibrate the name of the Archangel of Earth - Auriel (as you have been doing) then vibrate the name Phorlakh, the Angel of Earth.

The vibration of these names should cause changes to take place in the scenery and it should come alive, colors should appear more strongly. You may sense beings there and feel that one of them approaches you.

However do not, without further instructions, proceed to do any more than observe the "scenery" for now and for a long time. Your first requirement is to get familiar with the element and with passing thru the door easily. When this is attained you can contact me for further instructions or, by that time, your intuition will give you directions as to how to proceed.

To return to the outer earth plane from the inner earth plane you reverse the process. Step back thru the door and again feel yourself going thru the door and again feel it closing behind you. Make this return very definite and exact. Do not, for example, return suddenly by just opening your eyes and getting up physically. Keep the two planes separate and apart from each other. End the

91

work in the Inner and return to earth following a definite path or route.

Do not repeat this work-experiment too often especially at first. Take it easy. Consult your Moon Sign Book always and keep a record of the best times and those of the slow times especially. As said before advanced work along these lines is available and you should contact me before going further with this system.

You have, at your disposal, three other inner plane systems which will give you all the safe inner plane work you can handle for a long time; and to accomplish practically all you can want to accomplish for ordinary things and in ordinary magical work, especially work pertaining to your physical well being and practical work having to do with your material supply and I do mean money.

This last system is truly a deep inner plane system and can bring you into touch with the inhabitants of these Inner planes which the other three systems do not do except by accident. So stay away from too much of this advanced system until you are really ready to do this advanced work. Dealing with the inhabitants of the Inner planes is almost an Art in itself and has to be learned as were the other arts. They will not be of much use to you as you might think. These inhabitants are little more than personalized forces and dealing with them requires exact knowledge and techniques. They are not human in any way.

There are a few more applications of this symbol method that you can start using for now. Let us suppose you are seeking some special knowledge about a certain subject. You will have to find a symbol that represents that special knowledge. To find that symbol you will have to have a system of some kind in order to locate the exact symbol in relation to other things. The system I use, and teach, is the Caballa. In the Caballa system is a diagram called the "Tree of Life" On this tree is arranged all things. I find on this tree what thing I seek knowledge about and generally there are a number of symbols connected with that thing. I then make and color a composite symbol of the knowledge I am looking for (see above previously referred too lessons Change Name and Be a Power etc.) I then proceed to work with this symbol the same way as laid out in the preceeding instructions. I then carefully note what I see in the place I go to using the symbol as a door etc. The knowledge is very revealing.

You should make up a symbol of your astrological sign and of your plantary ruler and use them as doors to enter the Inner planes where they exist and thus learn all about them and become in tune with them. A very necessary part of your work.

Last Section

The whole object of this book has been to give you, an Occult student, a good practical start along the lines of Occult development.

In this book you were told that your life's happiness depended on your control of the physical circumstances which constitute your life, that is your physical life on this Earth plane.

You were told that it was possible for you, while living a physical life, to enter these Inner planes, under certain circumstances, and, after studying the Inner planes of causes, to alter causes so that effects, when they reached you on the outer physical plane, were conducive to your physical life instead of opposing it.

Also in this book you were shown-taught, by four different methods, how to enter the Inner planes.

You were not, however, given any further instructions on how to actually alter the aforesaid circumstances. I did not leave out these instructions for any reason other than the fact that altering circumstances is a very advanced type of work and it was first important that you should learn how to enter these planes FIRST. This was the first part of your work and you had to learn it first. I just could not handle beginning work and advanced work at the same time, in the same book. The subject is too vast.

I therefore recommend strongly that you strive, for now, to perfect the Art of projection. Learn all four methods and learn them well.

As your development with these four methods increases and you perfect your ability to enter the Inner planes, at will, a great deal of natural knowledge will come to you spontaneously. You should perceive the reasons for many things by your own observations and experiments. I have given you several leads already by use of which you can accomplish a great deal along making circumstances what you want them to be.

In all written Occult Knowledge (in contradistinction to oral teachings) even from as far back as 3000 years ago, —the Egyptian book of the Dead — on down to our own so-called modern New-Thought stuff, THE HOW OF THE INNER PLANES HAS ALWAYS BEEN THERE(how things are) IT WAS ALWAYS THE WHY THAT WAS MISSING (why do things work the way they do). In this book you have a great deal of the WHY. Many intelligent people cannot make the HOW work without knowing the WHY. In fact the more intelligent you are the more apt you are to not to be able to make the Inner plane stuff work. Or another way of saying it is that the more objective you are the more apt you are to misdirect the subjective. Both the objective and subjective parts of your being must be trained-forced to work with each other — the balance should be about equal — not too much of one or the other. If you are too objective you will become too skeptical of what you cannot "see" directly; and if you are too subjective you become too easily influenced by what you do "see" directly, and, in both cases you go off on the wrong track and end up where you do not want to be and doing something you do not want to do.

In this book (for the first time that I can find) you have been presented with a series of directional exercises which combined both the objective and the subjective phases of physical be-ing. The objective part of you was given a series of directions-exercises; presented to your intellect, in such a way, as to constitute a challenge to it to go ahead and find out what is true, in its own way which is the only way that will satisfy it. The subjective part of you was given a series of emotional experiences, generated by the objective part's operations, which emotional experiences satisfied many of the doubts latent in the depths of your being which doubts, being satisfied, you can go then ahead with confidence in your ability to handle your physical outer life in a more satisfactory manner which should lead to extended happiness in living. THUS MAKING THE HOW WORK!

I really should apologize. I DID NOT KNOW, AT FIRST, WHAT WAS GOING ON. I was led into the Occult, as explained in the dedication of this book but nothing else was explained to me.

When given the directions and material for this book I thought this was just a book on an interesting subject, but now it appears to be much more than that as you can, and will, see for yourself. This book is to be the first of a series of books on Occult subjects in which the Occult subjects are to be treated from the point where other writers-teachers leave off.

I hope you noticed this difference in this book from the other books on this subject of Astral projection and otherwise. Let us take the book called Astral Projection by Yram. (You will find this book listed on our list of research books, you should get it for your study.)

Yram tells all about HIS experiences and his experiments in Astral projection BUT HE DOES NOT TELL HOW TO DO IT. (He did it thru the symbol method). So what on earth good is this book to you, and your desire to learn this Art, if he does not tell HOW HE DID IT. Yram calls the method he used "An open secret" "known to all Occultists" Open indeed!!! Now that I have given you the method, and other methods too, you can profitably get and read Yram's book but before you had any method at all for learning HOW TO DO IT YOURSELF Yram's book was not worth a tinkers dam.

Or take Muldoon's book—The Projection of the Astral Body—Mr. Muldoon describes his experiences in some detail but he doesn't tell you exactly how to project for yourself; except to say that projection is done thru Will Power and Desire. In my humble opinion Mr. Muldoon is a natural projector and I don't know if he can teach others to project for themselves or not. I wrote to him years ago asking this question but I received no satisfactory answer to my question and so I made no further attempts to question him. However now that you possess directions as to how to do it yourself you can profitably read Mr. Muldoon's book and you will find it on the list of books that I will keep on supply for your convenience.

I have, at one time or another, tried to contact every known Occultist in the world that was living. I made many contacts but none of them were worth very much. I found out very little of value. THEY WERE ALL WHY MEN. AND THERE WAS NOT A HOW MAN AMONG THEM.

I was wondering if you came to the same conclusion as I had — that it appeared very hard to deal with the Occult in a satisfactory practical manner — that all Occult books seemed to be written by impractical psychic, mystics that either rapturize ordinary Occult laws-facts into a new kind of an emotional religion or become so vague that they cannot make themselves clear to anyone as to what they mean and why. Then there is another kind of writer that writes about the lives and works of the above mentioned Naturals and describes their born abilities which abilities they cannot pass on to you to TEACH YOU ANY WAY TO DUPLICATE THEM. And, as said before, what good are the other fellow's born abilities to you? except to merely read about them for general information. There is a book called "There is a River" which book is about Edgar Cayce. You will find it on our approved rearding list but only to give you some ideas as to what is going on in the semi-occult world.

I find myself repeating again what I said before that what students-people, who are deeply interested in Occult subjects, need, more than anything else, are good sound books containing factual "Why" Occult knowledge of workable theories AND GOOD PRACTICAL "HOW" DIRECTIONS AS TO HOW TO DO IT THEMSELVES. That is how to practice Occult knowledge so as to produce EFFECTS-RESULTS, ON THE PHYSICAL PLANE. Without results on the Physical Plane all mere knowledge and practices are worthless and valueless. Dion Fortune said in one of her books — "the power, coming down the planes, is to be grounded in Earth." and unless it is grounded it is just empty talk.

I am reminded of certain things I read about Aliester Crowley in a book called the Magic of Aliester Crowley by John Symonds. The author describes a series of invocations that Crowley goes thru in Paris in 1914. These invocations were addressed to Jupiter mostly and one of the things asked for was money. The results consisted of vision of various kinds but no money or very little. One gets the idea from this book that the invocations did not accomplish what was wanted of them, some money.

And the reason for no money is quite simple. According to the symbol of the Tree of Life of the Caballa system that Crowley was using, Jupiter is located on a high abstract plane, in fact this plane is called the archetypal plane, by Occultists. This plane is where the beginnings of things originates.

Well you can figure it yourself that if you are dealing with a force that "exists" only on a plane that has to do with beginnings of things only, how could you expect to get solid money from an invocation like that? No you would not get "solid" things, you would get only what the plane has to give and that would be archetypal ideas. When you want money you must invoke a God force that is much closer to earth than the archetypal plane. A God on the Earth plane. I hope to write other books that will enable you to understand these things better. There is no reason why you should not have the best of the Physical world and the best of the Inner world.

Until then you will have to depend on the books now available. I have no way of knowing now, of course, how much or how little Occult knowledge you students, reading this book, will have. Those of you who have done a great deal of study, and accumulated a library, will have an advantage over others who are just starting out on the path. However you will find, in the list of books recommended here in this book, those Occult books which, in the opinion of Ophiel, are the only worthwhile books available. To go with these books will be prepared summaries and expostulations which will give, in full detail, what the book means and what the author is saying. This should be of tremendous help to the student anxious to make solid progress along the path.

I suggest that you begin to systematically purchase these books, and the summaries thereof, and study them hard.

While you are doing this there are two additional Occult operations that you can pursue with great profit — one is to start your study of the great system of the Caballa, which you will be doing in the above mentioned books, and to assemble and draw and paint your magical tools centering around this great system.

The second thing for you to do is to start to learn and practice divination! There is a terrific amount of wrong thinking and wrong understanding about the subject— Art of Divination. I will correct as much of the misunderstandings as I can here and now.

Divination is not fortune telling. The Art of Divination is the Art of finding out, as correctly as possible, HOW AND WHAT THE PLAY OF THE COSMIC-FORCES-CYCLES is as of the moment-hour-day-week etc. What the Cosmic forces are is fully taught and explained in the Caballa system and many of you are familiar with these forces as they are taught in astrology which is not too bad but too much misunderstood for the use of the average person. These Cosmic forces are always moving one way or another thru the Cosmos, sometimes strong, sometimes weak. Sometimes pulling one way sometimes pulling or pushing another way. You might compare them with the winds that blow over the oceans. I do not know how much you know about sailing ships, I know nothing, but I can understand that the various sails on a ship can be set by means of ropes and other devices so that the ship can be put to the wind no matter, almost, from which direction the wind is coming from, can in fact, sail almost directly into the direction from which the wind is coming from.

So thus it is with these Cosmic forces that influence our lives so much. If you can accurately find out which way they are set you can trim your own sails so that you can move ahead even if there is opposition ordinarily making such a move impossible.

I have prepared for your study two systems of Divination. One system is as old as the Earth (also as old as the Element of Earth) This system is called Geomancy of Divination by means of Earth. And the other system is one that I discovered my self thru the use of the Tarot cards, or I should say rediscovered. I call this system the Oracle of Fortuna.

In both of these systems you will make some of your magic tools yourself. You can practice on the models that I will send you but for best results you must make your own tools. But the most important thing to do is to learn. To help you again on these two systems we will keep supplies on hand and/or full directions as to how to make the necessary magical tools.

For the Geomancy workings you will need a tray like box to hold the sand and various other kinds of sticks to make the marks with. This tray-box must be able to be closed and locked so that others cannot get easy access to it. You will have to paint it a certain color and in a certain way etc.

The Oracle of Fortuna will have to have a number of cards drawn and colored. And various other symbols drawn and colored. Although I rediscovered this system by using Tarot cards you will use an ordinary deck of cards for various reasons.

I suggest that as soon as you read this book for the first time that you establish contact with me thru the address given in this book. New things will be coming out all the time and it would be well to keep in touch with us.

Now I would like to discuss the question of money for my services. It always comes up that Occult Knowledge should not be sold but given away. And I agree with this. I make no doubt that there was probably a time in the olden days when this knowledge was in the hands of priests and temples and that it had to be guarded more closely than now. Probably the reason for this was that all ancient peoples knew about these things, more or less, instinctively and if some knowledge of the practices did get out into the wrong hands it could interfere with much legitimate work. This is not the same situation about Occult knowledge today. Occult knowledge can be used more freely now-a-days. In those days everyone KNEW there was something going on but the average man did not have the knowledge to understand these things. The average man could not even read. You did not have to sell anybody on the Occult in the old days, they all KNEW but there was no way the average man could learn these things except they were TAUGHT TO HIM by somebody. And they were not taught to everybody but only to those who passed the tests.

Thus, of course, the worst crime in the world was to teach the Occult knowledge to those who could not pass the tests, and teach them for money. Times are much different now. Now days the bulk of the people are completely ignorant of the powers of the Inner planes and they have to be sold on its use. Then too now days Occult knowledge will be used for entirely different things than it would have been used for in the old days. Today Occult knowledge is used in connection with natural forces and in the old days it would have been used AGAINST PERSONS TO INJURE THEM.

Today, in this material world, how on earth can anything be done without the exchange of money for services? Every church that I ever heard of asks for money to keep up its work. Every college that I know of takes tuition money from its students. I don't see how I could sell this book or find students if I did not advertise/announce for them. It is not as if I lived in a small town with a market place and I could go around and meet everybody every few weeks personally. Typewriters, stamps, paper supplies, are all gotten for money.

Then too there is the serious question of how many years I spent learning this Occult Art Knowledge. Years in which I did not do any profitable work earning money for which I was bitterly criticized by my family and relatives and others. I had a small income but it did not give me enough to be other than just on the edge of always needing something. I was driven to find the TRUTH ABOUT THINGS. I kept up until I did find out some truths and I did make some progress along the path. Now I can give positive directions to students about how to handle the Occult and the students can expect positive results, according to whatever natural ability they have to reproduce this Art in themselves.

Then too I have found that unless a thing has a price on it it is not considered to be worth very much. Generally too the higher the price the more valuable it is considered to be. I have tried to give this knowledge away and it was thrown back in my face!

I am going to respectfully suggest that you write to me one letter when you start on this book, enclosing one dollar to cover costs. Tell me all about yourself and how much you have studied, what books you have etc. You should receive the current issue of the Astral Light, a small publication that is still in folio form now but by then probably larger. The Astral Light will contain a great deal of sound occult knowledge. Announcements, evaluations of Occult Books, evaluation of moving pictures that have Occult significance or are based on Occult matters. Additional papers from me or from others or advanced students regarding results of Occult work Etc.

There is another matter that I'd like to take up here and get out of the way once and for all. This is the matter of "wrong" use or using Occult powers for "evil" purposes. Almost any release of real Occult knowledge, especially of the vital type as given in this book, will bring loud screams of anguish from old maids and old foggies that the knowledge and practices will be used for "wikkid" purposes etc etc. Just what are the possibilities of this happening?

Well the first thing that would seem to be to argue against this sort of thing is the obvious fact that only persons of a very low type of mind and tendencies would have any inclination to use these powers for evil purposes, what ever that means. My personal experience with this type of person is that you could not hire them with all the gold in Fort Knox to carry out physical evil actions using mental Occult powers. These persons would a million times rather work physically direct than resort to mental Occult indirect means; leaving out of consideration entirely the question as to their mental ability to accomplish anything along these lines thru mental Occult means, or their desire to do so.

In this connection I always recall a story that I heard — After the last war was over the armed services left, on a little island in the South Pacific, a large store of canned food. This food was turned over to the Chief and his people as a gift without, however, telling them how to get the cans open. The Chief, and his men, struggled for a long time to get that food out of the steel cans but was never able to do it successfully with their primitive tools.

The Chief racked his brains and finally remembered that he had seen the former owners using some stuff called dynamite to blow open the rocks and other things. He then took his boat and went to another island where there were still soldiers and he asked these soldiers to give him some dynamite and show him how to use it. The surprised soldiers asked him what on earth he wanted dynamite for and when he told them they laughed and gave him some can openers and showed him how to use them.

Now the point of this story is quite obvious — Why use dynamite to open a can of beans when a can opener will do a much better job and much easier? And so it follows too — why use high Occult powers to accomplish results when lesser physical-mental powers will do it and better and easier?

What then, in the first place, does a man turn to the acquirement of

Occult knowledge and of Occult powers for? I say he expects it to do something for him. To relieve him of some of the heavy burdens of Physical living. To make life easy and more abundant for him. Most people are very unhappy with this physical life. They are not wise as to how to get thru life properly and the average church is far from a help when it should be a source of knowledge and power to its members and followers. The ordinary church, having failed the man, he hears about Occult knowledge and Occult powers and he wonders if he could acquire some of these to help him thru life. The truth is that Occult knowledge and Occult powers can help you to improve your physical life BUT GENERALLY NOT IN THE WAY THAT YOU THINK IT WOULD. The application of Occult power has to be done as intelligently and correctly as any other kind of operation. Certainly not by using it as one would use dynamite to open a can of beans!!! What is the right way to apply Occult knowledge to the problems of life? The first step is to start on the path. Once started you cannot turn back, as all the books say, but the truth is that NO ONE EVER WANTS TO TURN BACK!!! Study and meditate. As you learn about the hidden things of Life that the Occult reveals to you and what it, Life, is really about you gradually learn to handle Life and to handle it properly. There comes a time when you "GO OVER THE LINE." These things are explained in a book called Cosmic Consciousness which you will find on our book list. This book has not too much value but you should read it once.

When once you have gone over the line you are then to become one of the self-born. Those who are consciously entering the Inner planes and living and working thereby.

Now, of course, this is what all the books say — and then leave you to find your own way with a dull thud, as you hit the bottom of something.

In the books that I write; and in the lessons that I give; you are not going to be treated to flowery phrases and descriptions of the "sacred" and "holy" things and have to read poetry about the inner things and such, or have to read rapture gush about the colors of the elemental forces as Jakob Bohme when he became clairvoyant enough to see them, but how in the heck do you use them? and that is the only important thing, not how beautiful they are etc.

In this book you have already received enough good sound practical, workable Occult knowledge to set you up for a better, more successful life than you would ever have thought possible for you before. So get going!!!!

One more thing and then I will be through with this section. Most everybody in the world suffers from a lack of Love. This is one of the most serious troubles that bothers humanity and, seemingly, one of the most difficult to handle. All I can say now is that you will have to suffer until you can develop yourself to the point when your own other-side of your own Inner being comes to the point when the secret, mystical marriage takes place between your own Inner beings and the true union is accomplished, or at least starts to become a living reality in your life. This life is never going to be perfect so don't look for it to be accomplished. There is nothing that can MAKE YOU HAPPY. You HAVE TO BE HAPPY.

Try to control the idea that some other person can give you happiness or the possession of some one certain person is the answer to happiness. Many people look for Occult powers to "get" some certain person in the mistaken belief noted previously. However if you will apply yourself study and go into it and deeply follow where it leads the time will come when you would not touch that former desired person with a ten foot pole and you will marvel how you could have ever thought differently.

The same with the desire for money. You will find that you will develop sources of money supply that will be your own and you will not want anyone's else money.

— SO MOTE IT BE —

Addenda

In the text of this book I said that I would give you a list of the only good Occult books which I have found to be of value to an Occult student. Many people have been very much disappointed that they could not get sound Occult knowledge and practices from Occult books; and many people have said to me that it was impossible to get Occult knowledge from Occult books and that Occult knowledge had to be gotten from some other source.

Well the above is both true and not true for the following reasons — Occult books generally contain two kinds of Occult knowledge. The first kind of knowledge will tell "WHY" and the second kind of Occult knowledge will tell "HOW", (or the books should contain the "HOW" along with the "WHY" but there is not too much "HOW" in Occult books for reasons that were explained before and will be repeated here again so that you will understand this throughly.) Forgive the repeat!

These two kinds of Occult knowledge are equally important — certainly it would be fantastic to give a person a line of learning-knowledge without telling him "WHY" AND "WHY" in detail. And it is certainly fantastic to give a man intensive Occult knowledge-information and then not go on and show him "HOW" to use the knowledge in a correct and practical manner.

Unfortunately, almost without exception, Occult books seem to be of the former type.

This strange anomaly was explained to you before, in this book, wherein I said that this was to due to the circumstances of an Occult teacher having received Occult training from a secret society under strong oaths of secrecy and all he can do for the rest of his life is blab about the Occult but never give any decent practical working directions. You must have noticed this. Dion Fortune comes right out and says it plainly in her books.

However, in spite of the above facts, we must still have Occult books, incomplete as they are. After all these books do contain information that is basic and vital for your foundational training in Occult knowledge.

Fifteen years ago I was refused admission to one of those so-called Secret Occult societies. I was very much surprised at the refusal of membership as I considered myself a devoted and hard working Occult student. After much pondering on this subject I concluded that I was much too independent for them and had showed it in my responses to their lessons and questions.

Now I am eternally grateful that I was not accepted for membership although at the time I was very much put out about it. I was forced, by their actions, to go ahead on, and by my own and this I did: later I made all the necessary Inner power contacts-connections that I will ever need for the rest of my life — more power than I will ever be able to use. I have material here that I will never be able to get written down as I don't think I will live long enough to do it.

However due to this fact, that I got the Inner plane connections myself, I am under no obligation to anyone for them, and I can give to students all the "HOW" teaching-practices and "HOW" Occult training that you can stand.

However basically tho you can, and will, still get your "WHY" knowledge from books now on the market and it is for this purpose that I call your attention to the following list of Occult books and authors which I have used and which I consider contain practical vital information. Some of these books are long out of print and not readily available. I will endeaver to have them, or copies of them, available for your study. All other books that are available on the market now I will carry here; again for your convenience in case you do not find yourself able to obtain them more easily where you live. (I wish I had had this service available to me when I was starting out 30 years ago)

The following list is fairly complete for your first studies. I have searched all over for every good Occult book that I ever heard of and these are the only good ones that I found. If you know of a book that is good and it is not on this list let me know about it and if it is good I will add it to the list later. Contact me for other more advanced books.

For beginners in the Occult I would recommend four books by a man and wife team named Richard and Isabella Ingalese. The books are "The History and Power of Mind." "Occult Philosophy," "Fragments of Truth" and "The Greater Mysteries," These books are for those who are absolute beginners in the Occult and know absolutely nothing about the subject. I do not regard them as the last word on the Occult by any means nor are you to stick with them too long, as I did, or you may have to unlearn some things. They are just good enough to introduce you to the Occult and leave you with a desire for more although some of their conclusions are a bit thin.

Another writer of books for beginners is William Atkinson. He wrote many books on the subject treating it in many different kinds of ways. In fact he wrote so many books that he had to take another name in order to go back over the same ground to piece together some things that he left out of the first books. His second name was, I think, Du Mont. Mr. Atkinson gives a lot of good practical encouragement to Occult students without giving too much of "HOW" but in this case it would be well to know what you might be expected to do after you have some Occult power. I was told, by a person who once worked with him, that in writing his books he would read for days and then start by setting down and writing off some lines on a piece of paper which paper was immediately taken and set up in type and final type at that! He never rewrote, or corrected, his work! As I said much good general information is there but not too deep or too profound. I will have his best books available here and some comments on them, as to what to look for and study.

By the time you have gone this far in your reading (and being in touch with me all the time I hope) you should be ready for Dion Fortune books which are as follows and should be read in this order—

Sane Occultism. Esoteric Orders and their Work. The Training and Work of an Initiate. Spiritualism in the Light of Occult Science. Through the Gates of Death. Psychic Self-Defence. The Mystical Qabalah. Cosmic Doctrine.

Novels. The Demon Lover. The Winged Bull. The Sea Priestess.

Secrets of Dr. Traverner, Moon Magic.

Dion Fortune sounds like a master of the Magic Art. Her books are full of "WHY" and some "HOW". I got a great deal out of Psychic Self-Defence and in there she actually gives some practices but the practices are things that are well known in Occult Circles. Also in her novels she gives a great deal in the way of practices in action as it were and the Occult student that is "ready" can get much from those books. Dion Fortune died somewhere around 1946 and I have not been able to find out much about her death circumstances. In fact I have been waiting for someone to write a biography of her but it has not been forth coming as yet. Some of the material in Psychic Self-Defence is autobiographical. She founded a Society called the Society of the Inner Light which is still in existence in London.

After you have gone thru some of Dion Fortune's works you can then also take up the works of Israel Regardie. Mr. Israel Regardie is a must writer for Occult knowledge along the lines of the Qabalah and in many ways the two writers supplement each other. At this date (1961) Mr. Regardie lives in Los Angeles and is working along Psychological lines.

Mr. Regardie has published many books of his own as well as edited and arranged the material of the Society of the Golden Dawn. One of Mr. Regardie's books, that is much sought after and has been long out of print, is the book called "The Tree of Life." This book is very useful to the Occult Student and should be read and studied by everyone who aspires to the Sacred Art. We will try to have this book back in print by the time you will want to get it. Another very good book by Mr. Regardie is "The Romance of Metaphysics." this book is still in print and, to my way of thinking, has been greatly overlooked by Occult students. Mr. Regardie told me that this book's sales have been very slow although this was some years ago. I found the book very helpful and I suggest that you get it at once. It is as good an Occult book as I have ever seen. Another little book by Mr. Regardie is the "Art of True Healing." also out of print but I hope to have it in print by the time you will need it.

The books of Aliester Crowley contain much very good Occult Material but their study should be postponed until you are well along in your work. Aliester Crowley was a very strange man and acted very strange in all his ways. However much that was said about him was not really true or greatly over exaggerated. In addition he had a very strange-strained sense of humor which was not understood, or appreciated, by 90% of the people. You have to have a very analytical type of mind and much patience to winnow the wheat from the chaff in his writings and it is for this reason that I suggest you defer the study of his works until you are well along in your development. I may make up resumes of his material later for your study in which I will leave out the junk. Most of the real good material is in Mr. Regardie's Golden Dawn anyhow.

The books above listed will keep you busy for quite a while.

As suggested, and directed, in the previous section contact Ophiel when you have finished reading this book if you want to go further into these matters.

Ophiel operates, and directs, a real Occult mystery school along the lines of the Western Tradition — that of the Quballa.

Unlike preachers (not doers) of other philosophies Ophiel's school is FOR YOUR BENEFIT and by BENEFIT Ophiel means NECESSARY MONEY SUPPLY FIRST and twaddle-talk later.

You shall know the Truth and the Truth shall make you free!!!!

Free!! Free from what????

Why Free from Truth, of course. Truth is ugly especially Nature's truth.

The only real Truth there is IS YOUR OWN TRUE INNER DESIRES OF WHAT YOU WOULD WANT YOUR PHYSICAL LIFE TO BE LIKE.

THAT TRUTH YOU CAN REALIZE AND YOU CAN

START TO REALIZE IT NOW BY STARTING TO USE THE TEACHINGS IN THIS BOOK. AGAIN SO MOTE IT BE AMEN!

Ophiel welcomes correspondence from those who are interested in Occult subjects and the Occult Arts. Ophiel will answer questions regarding Occult knowledge and will also give personal instructions in the Occult Arts as well as can be done by letters. Although Ophiel, in this book, asked everyone sending in a letter to enclose a dollar very few have done so. (students in foreign lands do not send money because of the difficulties in exchange) All such monies received go for normal expenses and don't worry about Ophiel getting rich from this source!! If you have no money then say so when you send in your letter-questions. Ophiel's address is........

Ophiel
114 Broderick St
San Francisco 17
California U. S. A.

In the future a change of address may be made to Los Angeles. If your letter is not delivered to the San Francisco address then, thru long distance telephone information, check the Los Angeles area listings for Mr. Edward C. Peach or Peach Publishing Co. or Ophiel. If this draws a blank then write to the distributor of this book Llewellyn Publications — 100 South Wabasha St. — St Paul 7 — Minnesota — U. S. A.

It is contemplated that in the near future an Occult-Society school, to teach the Occult Arts, will be started.

This School will teach the Occult Arts freely and hold nothing back nor will any oaths be required of students and they will be free to use their acquired Occult knowledge-powers in any way they see fit and not be trained just for the use of some society as heretofore. The first type of instructions will be strictly SELF-HELP, SELF-DEVELOPMENT, and SELF-ATTAINMENT MENTAL MAGIC, ENTIRELY FOR THE BETTERMENT OF THE STUDENT IN ALL WAYS AND, FOR THOSE WHO NEED IT, I DO MEAN PURSE WISE *FIRST*.

When the time opens up other Magic subjects will be added such as Correspondence Magic — Sympathic Magic — Natural Magic — and finally RITUAL MAGIC AND ALL THE VARIATIONS OF THE ABOVE.

Many students have written me to ask if they will be able to "step" out of their physical body, "turn around" and "see" their physical body "lying there" by means of the projection systems given in this book. As this body-viewing-operation seems to be of so much importance to so many I will here answer "yes" (subject to your personal-ability-achievement of course) and give the following information-directions as to how to do it. The body viewing operation belongs partly to the "little system" and partly to the "body of light method" and is of the etheric projection type. The operation is performed thus —

After you have gained some proficiency in "working" both the "little system" and the "body of light method" you can lay out the following arrangements — You should have a private room where you will not be disturbed. You should have a bed or a deep chair which will support the body during the operation. This done then arrange two viewing points in this room. These two viewing-points are very much like the stations you used in the "little system". One of these points should be over the bed or chair on which you will sit or lie and the other point should be on the opposite side of the room.

When all this has been arranged you then proceed about the same as you did with the "little system" You start by lying on the bed or setting on the chair and look across the room at your viewing-point-object. Then get up physically and cross over the room and look at your viewing point intently until you have every detail fixed firmly in your mind-memory.

When you have every detail of this first point firmly fixed in your mind then turn around and look at the other viewing point above your bed or chair. Cross back to this point and look at it intently until you again have every detail firmly fixed in your menory-mind. Then turn around and again look at the first point and walk back to it and view it again etc. Establish this path between these two points in your mind until you can recall them perfectly.

Continue this route both physically and mentally. Sometimes do the "route" both physically and mentally, sometimes do the route mentally alone. Do this route very much as you did in the "body of light" method.

It is inevitable that with time, desire, concentration, and will power the moment will come when you will cross the room in your body of light turn around and "see" your physical body.

Now don't try any tricks. Don't go making tests, especially this first time. And above all don't panic especially this first time. Just view your body, turn around and reenter it. Then go on to perfect your projection technique.

ANNOUNCEMENT

Other books by Ophiel now ready — REAL OCCULT DYNAMITE!

THE ORACLE OF FORTUNA — Contains a marvelously simple and uncanny system of Divination, based upon the Caballa, which can give you accurate answers to vital questions regarding your daily life activities. These answers can help you avoid trouble and guide you correctly in many useful ways. The book also contains much vital Occult Knowledge coupled with the HOW type of directions so characteristic of Ophiel's practical way of teaching Occult Knowledge. The Oracle of Fortuna is presented to you in a series of 12 lessons in manuscript form.

THE ART AND PRACTICE OF GETTING MATERIAL THINGS THROUGH CREATIVE VISUALIZATION by Ophiel — Here is Occult Dynamite indeed! You have heard that it is possible to get what you want thru an Occult Process of Creative Visual Thinking. This process works very well for some persons but does not work so well for others. For the first time in the History of this subject Ophiel has reduced Creative Visualization to an Art of which all can learn how to operate somewhat and many will succeed in operating beyond their wildest dreams! Ophiel teaches that the Art of Creative Visualization consists, basically, of Ten Laws which Laws, when reduced to practice, greatly increase your Power of using this Art to get what you want. Available from the distributors named below. Or direct from Ophiel.

GNOSTIC SOCIETY LESSONS by Ophiel — Ophiel has founded a school for the study of Occult Knowledge. Membership is open to all with no restrictions what so ever. The lessons of The Gnostic Society for Self-Development cover a wide range of subjects of great interest to the Occult Student. Write to Ophiel direct for further information.

THE ASTRAL LIGHT — Ophiel issues a little news paper called "The Astral Light" from time to time. It contains much Occult Dynamite. It also contains continued articles on the Cabbala, Alchemy, and Magic.

Dear Students

If you will color the diagrams on the insides of the cover you will add greatly to their value to you as magic instruments and you will also make this book most personally yours. I suggest you do this and after you do this do not loan the book to anyone else but keep it wrapped up, in a square of black silk preferably, when you are not studying it. To enable you to identify the paths (the circles are paths, too) look at this diagram. The paths are numbered rather strangely and not in what you would think as normal order. The diagram in the front of the book will be colored in what is called the King scale. The diagram in the back of the book will be colored in what is known as the Queen scale. These are somewhat the reverse of each other. I also suggest that you take your drawing and coloring kit mentioned in this book and make up a number of diagrams like these for practice. Take the compass and ruler and, using these diagrams as a guide, mark off the circles and lines for the paths. When you have done this and painted several of them and got the colors fixed in your mind, proceed to paint the first diagram in the King scale which is as follows:

Circle-Sephirah

1. White Brilliance
2. Light blue
3. Crimson
4. Deep violet
5. Orange

6. Clear rose pink
7. Amber
8. Violet-purple
9. Indigo
10. Yellow

Paths

11. Pale yellow (lemon)
12. Yellow (darker)
13. Blue
14. Emerald green
15. Scarlet
16. Red orange
17. Orange
18. Amber
19. Greenish yellow
20. Yellowish green
21. Violet

22. Emerald green
23. Deep blue
24. Green-blue
25. Blue
26. Indigo
27. Scarlet
28. Violet
29. Violet crimson
30. Orange
31. Scarlet orange
32. Indigo

116

To make Akasha Symbol

Take a 4×5 card. Take your ruler and divide the card down the middle the long way and divide it again the short way across the middle.

Take the ruler and measure over 7/8″ of an inch each side from the center point where the two lines cross in the middle of the card. Place a dot there. Take your compass. Place the sharp end on the end of the middle line where the line leaves the card. Put the other end on the dot that marks the 7/8″ point from the center. Draw a half circle to the top and bottom of the card. Repeat this from the other end of the middle line.

This double half circle is the Akasha symbol. You can paint it in 4 ways the same as you did the others. The colors are Indigo and deep amber. (a sort of yellowish brown, you'll have to look this color up on the charts.)

Morning
invoking

Start   Night Time
Banishing

Diagram A
(See page 54*)

Students — If you will color the Tarot Card on the other side you, again, will make this book your own most personally shown. By coloring this card you will make it come "alive" so much so the "effect" can be noticed by you, and others.

If you will contact Ophiel you can secure a full and complete set of paints etc. needed for coloring this card; as well as the two diagrams on the front inside cover and the back inside cover of this book. Also extra diagrams for you to practice on before you do the book ones if you feel you need some practice first.

Color the cards as follows in this order —

Sky and pool — blue. Leave little waves of white in the pool.

Fore Ground — grass green.

Ground near in front of the towers but back of the fore ground. dark brown.

Mountains — light lavender.

Towers — Light grey, windows white.

Cray fish — purple.

Path — yellow, moon yellow, yods in air yellow. Also each yod has in its power pointed corner end a small red yod. Make these carefully last.

Dog — Light brown.

Wolf — Dark grey.

Try not to paint over any line.

Diagram B

The Sephirah and Paths Queen scale —

Circle-Sephirah

1.	White	6.	Gold Yellow
2.	Grey	7.	Emerald
3.	Black	8.	Orange
4.	Blue	9.	Violet
5.	Scarlet-red	10.	Divide into 4 parts as shown.

           1.   upper   Citrine
           2.   lower   Black
           3.   right   Olive
           4.   left   Russet

Paths

11.	Sky-blue	22.	Blue
12.	Purple	23.	Sea-Green
13.	Silver	24.	Dull brown
14.	Light blue	25.	Yellow
15.	Red	26.	Black
16.	Deep Indigo	27.	Red
17.	Pale Mauve	28.	Sky Blue
18.	Maroon	29.	Buff flecked silver white
19.	Deep Purple	30.	Gold Yellow
20.	Slate Grey	31.	Vermillion
21.	Blue	32.	Black

You are going to notice a lot of repeats in these colors. Some of these colors are hard to find easily but we will have them in the kits mentioned. Follow some of your own ideas about these repeats and do some meditating on the idea. However many of you will have to wait until you have accomplished a great deal of research-study before all the meanings and uses of these colors will come to you. Do the colors now according to directions. You won't use them for a long time but when you are ready you will have them.

For more information write to:
    Ophiel
    2915 Lane Drive
    Concord, California 94518